For information, please contact:
DeShawn Fontleroy
Sport Performance Consultant
4829 NE MLK, Suite 100
Portland, OR 97211
www.sportsmastery.com

THE SCIENCE OF SPORTS MASTERY: PSYCHO-KINETICS

For all practical purposes, The Science of Sports Mastery discusses the connection between mind, movement, and success. It further likens the brain to a machine; in such that the brain is a tool that can be programmed like a machine. In his book The Computer and the Brain, Dr. John von Newman says that the brain possesses the attributes of both the analog and digital computer.

The secret to using this material is by actively experiencing the practice exercises to stimulate your nervous system and mid-brain. This book has been constructed in such a way to force the student to exercise his or her imagination. It's processes guides the student to learning, practicing, and experiencing, new habits of thinking, imagining, remembering, and acting in order to (1) develop and enhance the self-image and (2) using creative thought to bring success and happiness in achieving particular goals. Visualizing, creative mental picturing, is no more difficult than what you do when you remember some scene out of the past, or worry about the future.

The Science of Sports Mastery can help the scholar athlete get answers to problems, invent, write, explore new horizons in science, develop a better personality, perform outstanding on college exams, dominate opponents, enhance training, or achieve success in any other activity intimately tied to living a fuller life.

Science has confirmed what philosophers, mystics, and other intuitive people have long declared: every human being has been literally "engineered for success" by his creator. Every human being has access to a power greater than himself. This means "YOU."

FOREWARD

Does psychology have a rightful place in the development of athletes or sports in general? This question is constantly asked throughout the sports performance industry. There are classes in universities all over the world that have a curriculum centered on the topic of sports psychology. However, very few have developed a step-by-step approach towards mastering the mental preparation needed for performing at the highest level of competition or when everything is on the line.

DeShawn Fontleroy has not only taken initiative to develop athletes physically, but he's developed Sports Mastery. It's a program that addresses the topic of developing the athletes' mental preparation. He developed Sports Mastery to help athletes overcome barriers that inhibit performance. It features tools to help the athlete prepare for competition or overcome challenges in daily life. Athletes and individuals alike who enter the world of competition naturally set goals for themselves. These goals often determine how much success they really want to achieve. Unfortunately, there are negative factors that naturally get in the way of one's success. Negative factors such as the fear of failure, self-doubt, procrastination, poor time management, lack of leadership, and not accepting the role of accountability. DeShawn has developed a program that requires self-initiative, dedication, consistency, determination, and shear will to become better prepared in sport and life.

I've bought into the Sports Mastery program because it's helped me address some of my fears. In the future, I look forward to guiding my athletes through the Sports Mastery program. My biggest accomplishment as a student was earning a B.S. degree in Exercise Physiology. I was also fortunate to achieve great success on the football field as well. If I had access to the systematic presentation of Sports Mastery during high school, my collegiate opportunities would have been ten-fold. DeShawn presents a program that every coach from amateur to professional would benefit from. I am currently applying the lessons, assignments, and wisdom compiled in Sports Mastery towards my new life goals. My quest on becoming a profound strength and conditioning coach and business owner now has a deep focus with intense clarity. Sports Mastery has given me a great understanding to a process of success and has ignited my ability to say the hell with procrastination! I've put self-doubt in my rear view mirror and looked the fear of failure right in the eyes. Sports Mastery has empowered me to fight against all measures until I succeed and finally become the successful leader I know I am capable of!

Alex Jones, B.Sc - S.T.R.I.V.E. Performance and Fitness

I'm not going to tell you how to change. People don't change. I want you to trust who you already are, and get to the Zone where you can shut out all the noise, all the negativity and fear and distractions and lies, and achieve whatever you want, in whatever you do.

If you're aiming to be the best at what you do, you can't worry about whether your actions will upset other people, or what they'll think of you. — **Tim S. Grover**

TABLE OF CONTENTS

THE ATHLETE'S MANIFESTO

I WILL BE READY TO WORKOUT AT THE START OF THE SESSION

I will be on time to my sessions. In fact, I will be early and get myself ready in attire and attitude. I will warm up and mobilize myself beforehand to the best of my ability. I will go into the start of each session ready to be the best me.

I WILL KEEP A RECORD OF MY TRAINING, EVERY SESSION

This is my job, not my coach's. It allows me to gauge my progress and keeps me progressing. It saves me and my coach time and keeps us from guessing what has happened and what is fact. It is up to me to make sure I always know where I have been, so I always know where I need to be.

I WILL BE CONFIDENT

I will be confident in my abilities, but not arrogant about them.

I WILL BE HUMBLE

There are always things I don't know. And also plenty of things I don't know that I don't know.

I WILL DO THE WORK

I will work hard. I will do what is asked of me as best I possibly can. And I will work on my weaknesses in order to be a better athlete and person.

I WILL BE COURAGEOUS

I will encounter leaps of faith almost daily. I will take them with an open mind and a heart full of courage.

I WILL BE AMBITIOUS – I will push myself day by day, week by week, and year by year. I will push beyond my perceived expectations and limits.

I WILL BE OPEN TO CHANGE

I will be open to new ideas and concepts, whoever they come from, and even if they go against what I currently believe. I may not agree, but I will decide that with an open and considered mind.

I WILL BE COMPETITIVE

But mostly with myself. I will harness my competitive spirit in ways that are healthy, hearty, and contribute to making me a better competitor and a better human being.

I WILL PUT FORM FIRST

Before weight, before time, before distance, before anything else. I know that compromising on form is taking a chance on my future. I will train for tomorrow.

I WILL RESPECT MY COACHES

I know that my coaches do their best each day to bring out my best each day. I will respect and appreciate this and will treat them as such.

I WILL GIVE CONSTRUCTIVE FEEDBACK TO MY COACH

I realize that coaching is a two-way process and will give constructive feedback to my coach in a suitable manner. I appreciate this will help my coach understand me better and help us both improve. I understand that all feedback, both ways, is for our ears and our ears only.

I WILL QUESTION ALL ASSUMPTIONS

I will question all assumptions, respectfully and appropriately. Sometimes this will mean asking questions. Sometimes this will mean reading and researching. It will always mean filtering any and all information through my experience and drawing my own conclusions.

I WILL ENCOURAGE, AND TAKE PRIDE IN MY PEERS

I will take just as much pride in the success of my peers as I do in mine, if not more so. When I finish my workout, rather than gloat in my own success or wallow in my own pain, I will encourage others of all abilities, whether teammate or adversary.

I WILL MAKE MISTAKES AND LEARN FROM THEM

I know mistakes are going to happen, both in practice and in competition. I know I will lose sometimes. I will smile, learn, and take it all in stride.

I WILL BE ACCOUNTABLE FOR MY OWN ACTIONS

I will be proud of my wins and responsible for my losses. I will act graciously after both.

I WILL BE A POSITIVE EXAMPLE

Positive words breed positive actions, in me and in others. I will be positive in my words and my actions. I will be the person I want to be.

I WILL BE COACHABLE

I will put faith in my coaches. I will commit to all of the above to make sure that I am open and receptive to coaching that is provided to me in good faith and often voluntarily.

I WILL BE COMMITTED

I will make a commitment to myself, my teammates, and my coach to be the best I can be. And when I say I will do something, I will do it.

I WILL ENJOY MYSELF

Above all, I will commit to having fun, enjoying what I do, and spreading good spirit and good word.

YOUR SIGNATURE:_____

DATE:_____

SPORTS MASTERY

FEAR

DEALING WITH YOUR FEARS

Fear keeps us focused on the past or worried about the future. If we can acknowledge our fear, we can realize that we are okay. — **Thich Nhat Hanh**

FEAR- NOUN: FEAR; PLURAL NOUN: FEARS

1. an unpleasant emotion caused by the belief that someone or something is dangerous, likely to cause pain, or a threat. "drivers are threatening to quit their jobs in fear after a cabby's murder" 2. synonyms: terror, fright, fearfulness, horror, alarm, panic, agitation, trepidation, dread, consternation, dismay, distress;

HIGH ACHIEVERS ARE WILLING TO DO WHAT THEY FEAR

Fear is the most powerfully inhibiting force known to man. It restricts us, tightens us, and causes us to panic, forcing us to abandon our great plans of life. If we are not willing to do what we fear, then fear, not ourselves, is in control of our lives. The high achiever cannot afford to surrender control of his or her life to fear.

FEAR ABOUNDS

Psychologists tell us that fear is the most common emotion in our society today. There are six basic fears that most people have:

- Fear of rejection or criticism
- Fear of ill health
- Fear of poverty
- Fear of old age
- Fear of loss of a loved one — being left alone
- Fear of death — the foundation of all fear

Unfortunately, fear's power is amplified by fear itself. It works like this: The more you fear something, the more that fear intensifies, and the more paralyzing it becomes. In many ways, worry becomes a self-fulfilling prophecy. That which we fear tends to come upon us.

FEAR IS A FRAUD

Zig Ziglar, one of America's favorite motivational speakers and authors, states that fear is an acronym standing for "False Evidence Appearing Real."

Psychologists tell us that most of our fears are false and that worrying about them is unnecessary. The following is a reliable breakdown of the time that people spend on various worries:

- Things that will never happen..............40%
- Things that are in the past..................30%
- Needless concerns about one's health...12%
- Petty and miscellaneous cares.............10%
- Real and legitimate concerns................8%

Of the 8 percent of the worries that are real and legitimate, half of them are about things we cannot influence. Furthermore, by taking positive steps we can eliminate about 2 percent of the real dangers we face. Therefore, it makes sense to be concerned about 2 percent of our worries. When you understand the dynamics of fear, you can face it and conquer it.

DOUBT: THE TWIN BROTHER OF FEAR

"Our doubts are traitors and make us lose the good we oft might win," wrote Shakespeare in Measure for Measure. Doubt destroys faith — faith in ourselves and in God. We lose all of the power that faith can give to us when we allow doubt, the twin brother of fear, to over-whelm us.

We live in an age that worships science. However, the very nature of science is such that it causes us to doubt anything that we cannot see, hear, smell,

taste, or touch. Unfortunately, for many people this creates the kind of doubt which says that nothing is valid unless it can be proven scientifically.

We can be open both to scientific achievement and to realities that we cannot experience with our five senses. But when spiritual doubt takes hold of our lives, we become immobilized and cannot realize our potential. All high achievements require confidence, the antithesis of doubt and fear.

Fear is at work in most poor performances. It's time to learn how to recognize fear's various guises, understand the role you may be inadvertently playing in generating your fear, and take action to neutralize the performance-disrupting effects of the fear. Fear is probably the single biggest cause of choking in sports.

When you play not to lose, your fear makes you too careful. Worrying about the outcome further feeds your fears and makes you play tentatively. Performing tentatively will keep you stuck. Peak performance always comes out of a fearless, go-for-broke attitude. During such a performance, athletes don't think about the outcome. While winning maybe critically important to them, it's just not relevant at the time. Peak performance requires athletes to go all out at all times. Fear of losing or any other outcome-based fears during a performance can cause athletes to hold back. For example, a pitcher who is afraid of throwing another ball may slow down her arm speed to try to guide the pitch instead of throwing it. The result is often a slow, very hittable pitch.

This apparent lack of concern for the outcome highlights a paradox in sports and peak performance: To win, when it counts the most, you can't think about winning. To reach your goals, you must let go of them when it's time to compete. Put your commitment, caring, and outcome focus into long hours of practice, the tough sacrifices, and the day-to-day training. Keeping in mind your goals and dreams during practice helps you stay focused and motivated. It will help you keep going when every other part of you is begging to quit. Your goals help you care enough to do what it takes to be successful. However, a goal or outcome focus too close to competition will only feed your performance fears and interfere with staying loose and having fun.

*To beat fear, you must first recognize it within yourself, understand it, and then take action to neutralize it.

THE HIGH ACHIEVER'S ACTION PLAN

What fears are holding you back from great achievements in your life? What great goals might you attempt to reach, had you no fear? True motivation for the high achiever can only occur when fear is replaced. But replaced with what?

Fear can only be replaced with confidence. The word confidence comes from the Latin phrase con fideo, meaning "with faith." Fear is replaced with faith — faith in who you are, faith in your life's purpose, faith in where you are going. Don't be afraid to climb out of the rut. A truly interesting life is not possible without some risk.

Sit down and make a list of all the things you are afraid to do, within legal, moral, and spiritual limits. Then go out and deliberately make yourself do every one of them. Each time you confront fear, become sensitive to the atmosphere surrounding it. Keep your senses fully open to receive and record even the smallest details. Don't let fear block your sensory resources. Make a conscious effort to observe everything around you. By concentrating on the atmosphere in this way, you may be able to ward off the intimidation of the task ahead.

If you are to become a high achiever, you must be willing to transcend fear. If you step out and are willing to do what you fear, then fear will no longer control your life. You will be on your way to high achievement.

RECOGNIZING FEAR

Recognizing fear should not be too difficult. It's a good bet you've been afraid at one time or another in your life. Fear is a universal experience with both positive and negative consequences.

DEALING WITH FEAR AND ANXIETY:

Nothing in life is to be feared, it is only to be understood. **-Marie Curie**

PRINCIPLE 1 - F.E.A.R.

FEAR AND CHOICE

First and foremost, understand that you always have a choice about how to respond to and deal with fear. You can cave into it, struggle with it, accept it, or work around it. You always have a choice, a choice you can make again and again or that you can change based on your assessment of what is best for you.

REDEFINING F.E.A.R.

Knowing that you have a choice about how to deal with your fears, consider the following reframe. Think of F.E.A.R. as an acronym for False Evidence Appearing Real. FEAR takes unsupported premises about impending doom, amplifies them, and presents the alleged results as inevitable failure.

I envision unsupported fears as hot air balloons. Once we grab hold of them, we are flung all over the countryside, terrified, out of control, anxious and powerless. Yet we fail to notice that no one forced us to grab onto the balloon in the first place. How would it be to stay put, safe on the ground, while the balloons go off on their merry, scary way? If this image captures your imagination, play with it. Next time you have a fear attack, imagine a big hot air balloon touching down near you. Notice how tempting it is to grab on (or even to climb into) the basket, and then see yourself deciding to let it go. Watch the balloon careening over the landscape, while you remain, safe and sound, on the ground.

DEALING WITH FEAR: EXERCISE

Make a list of all of your fears, writing as fast as you can to block the internal censor. Include EVERY fear, however small or irrational. Then read them aloud, suspending judgment. Allow yourself to feel the fear without grabbing onto the hot air balloon. Notice that being afraid does not have to mean losing ground.

If it feels comfortable, share your list with your coach. Before sharing your list, explain that you simply want a witness, that you are playing with how it is to acknowledge your fears without being pulled off center by them. Be clear that you are not asking for help and that you do not need advice. You do not need to be fixed. Ask your coach to simply listen, and to acknowledge you for being conscious of your fears.

Whether you think you can or think you can't, you're right. **-Henry Ford**

2 TYPES OF FEAR: DEALING WITH FEAR AND ANXIETY:

PRINCIPLE 2- DISCERN TWO TYPES OF FEAR

When dealing with fear, it is helpful to realize that not all fears are created equal. W. Timothy Gallwey and Robert Kriegel devote an entire chapter to two kinds of fear in their book, Inner Skiing, which they call Fear 1 and Fear 2. Fear 1 magnifies danger and vulnerability while minimizing your sense of competence. In other words, Fear 1 is False Evidence Appearing Real.

Fear 2 mobilizes your whole being for effective action. It includes a series of marvelous physiological changes that prepare the body for peak performance. Fear 2 focuses attention, provides adrenaline for extraordinary effort, and sharpens perception. Fear 2 promotes effective action, Fear 1 paralyzes us and prevents action.

EXERCISE

Return to the list of fears that you made in the first exercise in this guide. Now, you have the opportunity to sort your fears by type. Work through your list, labeling each fear as:

- Fear 1
- Fear 2
- Not sure, or includes aspects of both types of fear.

If you have not yet written a fear list, do so now. Writing down your fears is a powerful step in dealing with fears and anxiety and eventually managing them. Until you write them down, they are like so many vehicles in gridlock. Once you have them on paper, you can park some and move others, clearing a space for forward movement. In this way, writing down your fears creates a space for awareness and choice. (Tip: Refrain from judging yourself or your fears. Just list and label them.)

MAKING THE DISTINCTION BETWEEN TWO TYPES OF FEAR

Once you have a list, notice where Fear 1 and Fear 2 show up. The following distinctions will help:

- **Fear 1** promotes panic and confusion. **Fear 2** promotes clarity and purpose.
- **Fear 1** is often about saving face. **Fear 2** is about stepping out of your comfort zone.
- **Fear 1** triggers avoidance of the facts. **Fear 2** heightens awareness and perception.
- **Fear 1** wants you just to stop. **Fear 2** wants you to move forward powerfully and safely.

- **Fear 1** magnifies danger and vulnerability. **Fear 2** calls on our capacity to respond to danger.
- **Fear 1** originates in our ego mind. **Fear 2** is a whole-system response.

Both types of fear are present in many situations. What is important is to use your powers of assessment and discrimination to turn down the volume on Fear 1 while calling on Fear 2 for the energy and focus to move forward. With practice, you can actually transform Fear 1 into Fear 2 by focusing and accurately assessing the real risk and your real competence.

For example, Fear 1 makes a terrified skier (and I speak from experience!), see a shear drop where the slope is actually quite moderate. When the skier stops and measures the actual slope by holding her pole parallel to it, she increases her awareness of actual conditions, reducing the influence of Fear 1. By continuing to examine the slope, seeing in her mind's eye how she would ski the slope if she chose to, she further reduces panic. When at last she takes off down the hill, trusting in her competence and in her assessment of the challenge, she completes her shift from Fear 1 (panic) into Fear 2 (concentrated exhilaration).

Learning to deal with fears in this manner takes practice. The pay off is potentially unlimited as you remove barriers to learning, performance and joy.

NOTES:

ARE YOU CHALLENGED OR THREATENED?:

THE ANSWER GREATLY AFFECTS YOUR PHYSIOLOGY.

Under challenged, please create a list of thoughts you notice when you interpret your sport situation as challenging. Under threatened, please create a list of what you notice when you interpret the sport situation as threatening. One of the worksheet's goals is to help illustrate how your mindset affects your body.

CHALLENGED

- Heart rate settles down

- Lungs expand

- Heart pumps more blood, delivering more oxygen

EX: When I think. "This is my time! It is an opportunity to prove to everyone I can play!" I notice my body has more energy and I can breath normally.

THREATENED

- Blood preassure goes up

- Glucose is burned off immediately

- Fatigue sets in

- Poor decision making

EX: When I think, "All eyes are on me. This sucks" I notice my legs feel heavy and my breath is really shallow.

NOTES:

SPORTS MASTERY

MAKE THE MOST OF SETBACKS

E (event) + R (response) = O (outcome)

The basic idea is that every outcome you experience in life (whether it is success or failure, wealth or poverty, health or illness, intimacy or estrangement, joy or frustration) is the result of how you have responded to an earlier event or events in your life.

IF YOU DON'T LIKE THE OUTCOMES YOU ARE CURRENTLY GETTING, THERE ARE TWO BASIC CHOICES YOU CAN MAKE.

1. You can blame the event (E) for your lack of results (O). In other words, you can blame the referee, the weather, a teammate, your parents, the coaching staff, racism, gender bias, the lack of support, the political climate, the system, and so on. If you're a golfer, you've probably even blamed your clubs and the course

you played on. No doubt all these factors do exist, but if they were the deciding factor, nobody would ever succeed.

Lots of people overcome these so-called limiting factors, so it can't be the limiting factors that limit you. It is not the external conditions and circumstances that stop you –it is you! We stop ourselves! We think limiting thoughts and engage in self-defeating behaviors. We defend our destructive habits (such as drinking and recreational drugs) with indefensible logic. We ignore useful feedback, fail to continuously educate ourselves and learn new skills, waste time on trivial aspects of our lives, engage in idle gossip, eat unhealthy food, fail to train, fail to study, avoid necessary conflict, fail to tell the truth---and then wonder why our lives don't work. But this, by the way, is what most people do. They place the blame for everything that isn't the way they want it on outside events and circumstances. They have an excuse for everything.

2. You can instead simply change your responses (R) to the events (E) ---the way things are ---until you get the outcomes (O) you want. You can change your thinking, change your communication, change the pictures you hold in your head (your images of yourself and the world) ---and you can change your behavior---the things you do. This is all you really have control over anyway. Unfortunately, most of us are so run by our habits that we never change our behavior. We get stuck in our conditioned responses. We are a bundle of conditioned reflexes that operate outside of our control. You have to regain control of your thoughts, your images, your dreams and daydreams, and your behavior. Everything you think, say, and do needs to become intentional and aligned with your purpose, your values, and your goals.

SPORTS MASTERY
SUCCESSFUL HABITS FORMULA

IF YOU DON'T LIKE YOUR OUTCOMES, CHANGE YOUR RESPONSES

3 Steps to take in response to setbacks and adverse events:

1. Press Pause – absorb the experience and any bad news, journal your thoughts and feelings
2. Get your mind right - break down game film systematically, visualize game situations, practice with a ferocious game like intensity.
3. Step up – Make a point to stay focused, execute your roll and responsibility to the highest level. Make every effort to dominate the next opponent.

THE SUCCESSFUL HABITS FORMULA

This is a step-by-step method to help you create better habits. It works because it's simple. You don't need complicated strategies. This template can be applied to any area of your life, athletics or personal. If applied consistently, it will help you achieve everything you want. There are three fundamental steps:

1. CLEARLY IDENTIFY YOUR BAD OR UNPRODUCTIVE HABITS

It's important that you really think about the future consequences of your bad habits. These may not show up tomorrow, next week or next month. The real impact could be years away. When you look at your unproductive behavior one day at a time, it may not look so bad. The smoker says, "What's a few cigarettes today? It helps me relax. I'm not wheezing and coughing." However, the days accumulate and twenty years later in the doctor's office, the X-rays are conclusive. Consider this: If you smoke ten cigarettes a day for twenty years, that's seventy-three thousand cigarettes. Do you think seventy-three thousand cigarettes could have an impact on your lungs? Of course! In fact, the consequences can be deadly. **So when you examine your bad habits, consider the long-term implications. Be totally honest. Your career or life could be at stake.**

2. DEFINE YOUR NEW SUCCESSFUL HABIT

Usually this is just the opposite of your bad habit. In the smoker's example it would be, "Stop Smoking." What are you actually going to do? To motivate yourself, think about all the benefits and rewards for adopting your new successful habit. This helps you create a clear picture of what this new habit will do for you. **The more vividly you describe the benefits, the more likely you are to take action.**

3. CREATE A THREE-PART ACTION PLAN

This is where the rubber meets the road. In the smoking example there are several options. Read how-to-stop-smoking literature. Start hypnosis therapy. Substitute something else when the desire for a cigarette arises. Place a bet with a friend to keep you accountable. Start a fresh air exercise program. Use a nicotine patch treatment. Stay away from other smokers. The import thing is to make a decision about which specific actions you are going to implement.

You must take action. Start with one habit that you really want to change. Focus on your three immediate action steps and put them into practice. Do it now. **Remember, nothing will change until you do.**

ACTION STEPS: SUCCESSFUL PEOPLE I WANT TO INTERVIEW

THE SUCCESSFUL HABITS FORMULA

Make a list of athletes/people you respect, who have already done extremely well. Set a goal to invite each of them to breakfast, or lunch, or book an appointment by phone or in person. Remember to take a notebook or a tape recorder with you to capture their best ideas. Inquire about their successful habits and any tools used to create or enhance success.

NAME	EMAIL/ PHONE	INTERVIEW DATE

Look at the following example. There are three sections –A, B and C. In section A, define the habit that is holding you back. Be specific. Then consider the consequences if you keep on repeating this behavior. Every action you take has consequences. Bad habits (negative behavior) produce negative consequences. Successful habits (positive behavior) produce benefits and rewards.

In section B, define your successful new habit. Usually all you need to do here is write the opposite of what you had in section A. If your bad habit was arriving just as practice starts, your new habit could be arriving

30 minutes before practice starts. In section C, list the three action steps you will take to turn your new habit into reality. Be specific. Pick a start date and then get going!

A. Habit That Is Holding Me Back

EXAMPLE: Arriving at practice just as it begins.

CONSEQUENCES: Missing pre-practice focus points and strategy for upcoming opponents

B. Successful New Habit

EXAMPLE: Arriving at practice 30 minutes early.

BENEFITS: Better focus, pre-practice preparation, comprehensive instruction and game strategies received and understood.

C. 3-Step Action Plan to Jump-Start MY New Habit

1. Find a teammate to hold each other accountable for arriving 30 minutes earlier each day at practice

2. Set up weekly visits with coach to reflect on leadership role and responsibility

3. Make a list below of successful new habits & eliminate bad habits

Start Date: _____

A. Habit That Is Holding Me Back

EXAMPLE: Allowing distractions and interruptions throughout the day at school. Texting in class.

CONSEQUENCES: Missing key points to lectures, test scores dropping, increased stress, longer study hours, reduced social activities.

B. Successful New Habit

EXAMPLE: Giving my teacher undivided attention throughout class, only discussing course work in class, raising my hand to ask questions when I don't understand a topic.

BENEFITS: Able to complete assignments on time, quality/efficient study time, better exam scores, reduced stress, more time for social activities

C. Three-step Action Plan to Jump-start my New Habit

1. Write up a strategy to stay focused during class

2. Review strategy with instructor and parents

3. Monitor progress with instructor and exam scores

Start Date: _____

On a separate sheet use the same format to record your own habits and action plans. DO IT NOW!

A. Habit That Is Holding Me Back

B. Successful New Habit

BAD HABIT:

NEW HABIT:

CONSEQUENCES:

BENEFITS:

THREE-STEP ACTION PLAN TO JUMP-START MY NEW HABIT

1.

2.

3.

THREE-STEP ACTION PLAN TO JUMP-START MY NEW HABIT

1.

2.

3.

THREE-STEP ACTION PLAN TO JUMP-START MY NEW HABIT

1.

2.

3.

THREE-STEP ACTION PLAN TO JUMP-START MY NEW HABIT

1.

2.

3.

THREE-STEP ACTION PLAN TO JUMP-START MY NEW HABIT

1.

2.

3.

THREE-STEP ACTION PLAN TO JUMP-START MY NEW HABIT

1.

2.

3.

SUCCESS AND FAILURE CYCLES

A positive belief always propels you toward success. If you expect to win, you treat failures, obstacles, and injuries differently than if you expect failure. When things get tough, you simply become more tenacious. You refuse to quit. Set backs further fuel your motivation and determination to succeed. Your positive belief sets up a "self-fulfilling prophecy" in which you end up getting what you expect. Because you believe you can, you do. The success that you finally earn confirms and strengthens your original positive beliefs. Thus, a success cycle is set into motion. Because you believe you can, you do; and because you do, you believe you can.

Athletes in the middle of a winning streak demonstrate a simple, positive relationship:

Positive Expectations >>> Success >>> Positive Expectations

Athletes in the middle of a losing streak or poor performances demonstrate a negative relationship:

Negative Expectations >>> Failure >>> Negative Expectations

THE STRUCTURE OF BELIEF

When planning your assault against poor performance, you need to know as much about the enemy as possible. What are your negative beliefs? How are they constructed? What feeds them? Do they have any weaknesses? What weapons will be most effective in removing them? Are any of these available to you now?

If self-limiting belief is the enemy, what do we know about it? First, we know that belief is a conviction that

PERFORMANCE GRAPH

POOR PERFORMANCE

FEELINGS: NEGATIVE

ADDITIONAL FOCUS: SHIFTING

ENERGY: VARYING TO LOW

PEAK PERFORMANCE

FEELINGS: POSITIVE
ADDITIONAL FOCUS: IN THE PRESENT
ENERGY: HIGH

AVERAGE PERFORMANCE

FEELINGS: POSITIVE

ADDITIONAL FOCUS: SHIFTING

ENERGY: MEDIUM TO VARYING

certain things are true. It's a mental acceptance of this truth, even though evidence doesn't support absolute certainty. For example, a soccer coach got his team to believe that they always played better whenever the weather and field conditions were terrible. In the beginning of the season, he renamed his team "Mickey's Mudders" to reflect the belief he wanted to cultivate. When the skies opened up and the field turned to mud, their play always showed. He was tired of listening to complaints like "We need better field conditions to play our game," "We can't play in the mud," and "When the field is slippery, we always lose." He knew that his team's negative beliefs adversely affected its play in these situations.

There was little, if any, absolute truth in what coach Mickey was saying. The truth lay in how his players performed once they bought the belief that he was selling. While they played great under sunny skies, believing they played even better in the rain kept them calm and confident whenever the weather turned foul. Mickey said, "At first it didn't matter if it was really true that they played better in the mud. All that mattered was that they all believed it. Once they believed it, they actually began to play better."

To break down the walls of self-limiting beliefs and replace them with performance-enhancing ones, it would be useful to know how that wall is put together. As illustrated in the pyramid, beliefs have their base in the experiences that you have in and out of sports. But it's not the experiences per se that are important as much as the self-talk about these experiences. It's not how you play, what mistakes you make, or what the fans yell at you that shape your beliefs, but how you interpret these things to yourself. Beliefs really get their start with your self-talk. Finally, your beliefs impel you to action.

BREAKING DOWN

NEGATIVE BELIEFS

1. Change the Experience

2. Change Self-Talk

3. Change the Time Frame

4. Reframe Negative Beliefs

MAKING YOUR SETBACKS TEMPORARY

The left column contains examples of negative self-talk following a failure or setback. This self-talk reflects a permanent time frame and feeds negative beliefs. By altering the wording, make each sentence reflect a more temporary explanation of the failure or mistake. Sample answers appear at the end of the exercise.

PERMANENT	TEMPORARY
EXAMPLE: Why can't I ever swim fast when it counts?	EXAMPLE: I had a really bad race this morning.
1. We always blow the big lead.	
2. Whenever I try my best, I come up short.	
3. The coach never plays me.	
4. I just can't do it.	
5. They're impossible to beat.	
6. I'm a total head case.	
7. Our captain is unfair.	
8. I can't play in the wind.	
9. The referees are blind and unfair.	
10. Why bother; coach never listens to me anyway.	

The following sample answers represent only one of many ways that you could rephrase each statement in "temporary" terms.

1. We had a chance to win today and let up. We gave them one too many chances.

2. I gave it everything I had, but it wasn't enough today.

3. The coach needed the hot hitters in the lineup today.

4. I haven't been able to do it yet.

5. They have a good team, but we really improved in practices this week.

6. I let my nerves get the better of me this time.

7. The captain made an unfair call in that situation.

8. The wind distracted me today.

9. The refs made a bad call on that play.

10. I'm not sure coach heard what I said; perhaps I need to say it differently next time.

MAKING YOUR SUCCESSES PERMANENT

In the following examples of self-talk used to explain away a poor performing athlete's successes, change the language from temporary to permanent. Sample answers appear at the end of the exercise.

TEMPORARY	PERMANENT
EXAMPLE: We were so lucky to win.	EXAMPLE: We play really well together.
1. No wonder I won; I had no competition.	
2. Yeah, but he sprained his ankle in the tryouts, which is why I made the all-star team.	
3. My opponent got kind of tired at the end.	

4. No one really saw me coming; otherwise, I doubt that I would've been able to sneak a score.	
5. (jokingly) We paid the refs off; that's why we won.	
6. They just weren't used to playing in front of such a large crowd and we were.	
7. Someone was watching out for me today. Talk about freak occurrences!	
8. Their best player couldn't play today.	
9. Our defense got lucky.	
10. The judges were a lot harder on the earlier competitors than they were on me.	

The following sample answers represent only one of many ways that you could explain the success in permanent terms.

1. I won because I trained hard and was ready. I deserved this victory.

2. Even though he sprained his ankle, I was giving him the toughest match he'd ever had. I belong in this round.

3. I'm in fantastic condition.

4. My game plan is perfect and it wouldn't have mattered what my competition knew or didn't know I was planning.

5. We're a better, more disciplined, closer team…and we wanted it more.

6. We know how to stay cool under big-game pressure.

7. I made the breaks I got today. I create my own luck.

8. We can beat anyone they put out there.

9. We have a tough team and our defense is awesome!

10. The judges know a class act when they see it.

STOP NEGATIVE THOUGHTS

Turning negative self-talk into a more positive dialogue will ultimately weaken the negative beliefs that keep you stuck. Thought-stopping is a skill you can practice in training and before competition. The five-stage process listed below will help you first recognize that you're entertaining negativity, and then interrupt it and turn it around in a positive way.

1. Address the negativity as quickly as possible.

2. Say "stop" loudly to yourself.

3. Take a slow, deep breadth imagining that, as you exhale, you can breathe the negativity far away from you.

4. Reframe the negative thought into a positive one or change the time frame of the thought from permanent to temporary.

5. Refocus your concentration on the task at hand.

MAKING LEMONADE

Use the lemonade strategy to reframe the following examples of negative self-talk. Sometimes you may have to really stretch your thinking to come up with anything positive. If you're currently stuck in a slump, you're probably well-practiced in being negative. Trying to find the positive reframe may be difficult at first. Don't worry if you don't believe the reframe immediately. Just get in the habit of making lemonade. Be creative here to find the opportunity hidden in the problem. Sample answers appear at the end of the exercise.

ORIGINAL	REFRAMED
EXAMPLE: I hate playing in the rain.	EXAMPLE: The rain is going to upset my opponent more than me. I can use it to get an edge.
EXAMPLE: We look sloppy in warm-ups. This is going to be bad.	EXAMPLE: We'll have the jitters out by game-time and then we're gonna ball out!

1. What a terrible mistake to make! And so early in the contest. It's gonna be one of those days.	
2. They are so much taller than we are.	
3. This crowd is really huge!	
4. They have two all-conference athletes on their squad. We're in big trouble.	
5. It's so cold I can barely feel my hands and feet. How does coach expect us to play in this weather.	

The following sample answers represent one of many possible ways to reframe the negative self-talk.

1. No problem. Now that I've got that mistake out of the way I can really relax and look forward to playing well the rest of the game.

2. We're faster and smarter and will catch them off guard.

3. This is a great opportunity practice staying focused.

4. What a great opportunity to show what we can do against such good athletes. They probably won't take us seriously, which will really work to our benefit.

5. The cold is great. Look at what it's doing to everyone else's concentration. I can just relax now and use the cold to focus even more.

SPORTS MASTERY

THE POWER OF FOCUS

THE POWER OF FOCUS

Every champion athlete focuses on his or her unique talents and continually refines them to an ever-higher level of performance. No matter which sport you choose, the big winners all have one thing in common. They spend most of their time focusing on their strengths, the things they are naturally good at. Very little time is wasted on unproductive activities. And they practice, practice, practice, often several hours every day, honing their skills.

It's important to clearly differentiate your areas of brilliance from your weaknesses. You are probably good at a lot of things, even excellent in some. Others you are competent at, and if you are honest, there are some things you are totally useless at doing. On a scale of one to ten, you could plot your entire range of talents, one being your weakest

and ten being your most brilliant. All your biggest rewards in life will come from spending the vast majority of your time in the areas that score a ten on your talent scale.

To clearly define your areas of brilliance, ask yourself a few questions. *What do you do effortlessly – without a lot of study or preparation? And what do you do that other people find difficult? They marvel at your ability and can't come close to matching it. What opportunities exist for your areas of brilliance? What opportunity could you create using your unique talents?*

We are all blessed with a few God-given talents. A big part of your life is discovering what these are, then utilizing and applying them to the best of your ability. The discovery process takes years for many people, and some never truly grasp what their greatest talents are. Consequently, their careers are less fulfilling. These student-athletes tend to struggle because they spend most of their time in positions or on teams not suited to their strengths. It's like trying to force a square peg into a round hole. It doesn't work and it causes a lot of stress and frustration.

Deep practice reveals and unlocks brilliance. The power of focus works. Make it a part of your everyday plan and you'll experience dramatic jumps in productivity and self-improvement. We have a practical method that will make this easy for you and will also clarify your unique talents. It's called the Priority Focus Workshop, and is outlined at the end of this section. You need to be absolutely clear about what really goes on during your typical week in regard to training, competition, and academics. This reality check is usually very revealing. Basically, you make a list of all the activities you do around academics, competition, and training.

ACTION STEPS: THE PRIORITY FOCUS WORKSHOP

A PRACTICAL SIX-STEP GUIDE TO MAXIMIZE YOUR TIME AND PRODUCTIVITY

A. List all of the activities around academics and sports that use up your time.

For example: studying, practice, competitions, training camps, clinics, SAT Prep, meetings, study groups. Include everything, even the five-minute tasks. Be specific, clear and brief. Use additional paper if you have more than ten.

Describe four things that you are brilliant at doing in academics and sport.

1.

2.

3.

4.

Name the four most important things that enhance your success in academics and sport.

1.

2.

3.

4.

Name the four most important academic and training activities that you don't like to do or are weak at doing.

1.

2.

3.

4.

Name 4 people or organizations that could help improve these for you.

1.

2.

3.

4.

What immediate benefits will result from the Priority Focus Workshop?

What long-term benefits will result from the Priority Focus Workshop?

SPORTS MASTERY
FINDING YOUR PURPOSE

The Challenge

Let others lead small lives,

but not you.

Let others argue over small things,

but not you.

Let others cry over small hurts,

but not you.

Let others leave their future

In someone else's hands,

but not you. **-Jim Rohn**

FINDING YOUR PURPOSE

Are you wandering about with a lack of purpose in your own life? The ideas in this chapter go far beyond the specific daily habits you have started working on, important though these are. Now is the time to define a new meaning to your life. Let's figure out what's most important to you right now and get determined to making a difference.

Adopting a lifestyle that is on purpose provides an opportunity to enrich yourself and others. Now is the time to ask, "What am I doing with my life? What is my life's work all about? What legacy will I leave behind when my time is over?"

THREE KEY POINTS

1. Align your purpose with your natural ability.

2. Be determined.

3. Maintain a humble attitude.

Most people do not have a well-defined purpose. To help you figure out yours, here are some probing questions. Take your time to think through these before answering. If you are feeling stuck, or going through a major transition, consider taking a couple days off and retreating to yourself. Block out 2-3 hours, turn off your phone, shut down the computer and work through the following questions. It's impossible to make excellent decisions when you are caught up in the busy whirl of everyday activities. You can't think on the run!

Here are some key considerations: Your quest begins with recognizing your special skills and talents. What do you do best academically and from an athletic standpoint? What do you really enjoy doing? Most people stagnate academically and as athletes. They end up bored and just going through the motions. It's very frustrating. Often, the reason is a lack of challenge. The academic course load doesn't utilize their strengths. The position on the team doesn't utilize their strengths. Their energy is depleted and this individual is left uninspired. Does this in any way describe you or someone you know?

Purposeful work also means that you care deeply about something. You don't feel obligated to study or train, rather you're passionate about it. When you are living on purpose you feel that you are making a difference; you don't need to be popular or famous. You can make a significant impact in your academic community and on your team. Another important factor as you explore your direction is your level of enthusiasm. Are you in Have-To mode most of the time, or Choose-To? Living in Choose-To gives you power. You feel energized. When serving a purpose larger than yourself, your level of commitment also expands. As your purpose unfolds, you will develop a unique philosophy about life and a Big Picture viewpoint. Surface and routine tasks become less important as your work takes on new meaning. In order to live life to the fullest, your goals need to reflect your purpose.

SAMPLE PURPOSE STATEMENTS:

1. My purpose statement is, *To help as many student-athletes in my community, in a way that significantly improves their lives.* This gives me a multitude of opportunities. I can serve as a catalyst to create study groups for college entrance exams. I can also share my training ideas and routines with young athletes in my community.

2. My purpose statement is, *To inspire and*

empower fellow students to live their highest
vision in a context of scholarship and community.
I can join student committees, run for class president
or assist other candidates, give speeches, motivate
and mentor younger students, write articles, or
simply inspire the person sitting next to me in class.

3. My purpose statement is, *To inspire my
teammates with wisdom that will help them
perform better.*

4. My purpose statement is, *To take classes that will
prepare me for college and life after high school.*

LIFE'S FUNDAMENTALS

Know what you want
Know why you want it

Discover your talents
Use them daily

Work hard
Work smart

Find your purpose
Live your purpose

NOTES:

ACTION STEPS: DISCOVERING AND LIVING YOUR PURPOSE

The ten questions below were formulated to help you determine if your life is centered around purpose. In combination with the key points in this chapter, they will help you clarify a definition of purpose that works for you. Before responding, think about each question and read the comments. Then simply check "yes"; "don't know/not sure"; or "no."

1. Do you recognize what you are good at and what energizes you?

Yes   don't know/not sure   No

Many people never find their niche because they avoid analyzing their career objectives. They fall into degree programs and positions never asking themselves, "What do I do well? What type of life do I want to lead? What type of work creates positive energy for me?" It's important for you to know and use your special skills.

2. Do you fully utilize your most-enjoyed skills?

Yes   don't know/not sure   No

Many people stagnate in their jobs or sports career. They are capable of doing so much more, yet they are afraid to challenge themselves.

3. Does your studies/degree further some interest or issue that you care deeply about?

Yes   don't know/not sure   No

Caring is the basis of all purpose. It requires an openness to everything around you. To develop care, you need awareness. You should not be burdened by a sense of duty or obligation. When you care naturally, it's because something has profoundly touched and moved you.

4. Do you see yourself, through work, as making a difference in the world?

Yes   don't know/not sure   No

The "rust-out syndrome" is prevalent in today's society. Because so many people find work to be meaningless, they lose motivation. Work must offer more than money and status; it must offer you the chance to make a difference.

5. Do you view most days with a sense of enthusiasm?

Yes   don't know/not sure   No

When you are serving a purpose larger than yourself, you will feel more committed and become more enthusiastic.

6. Have you developed your own philosophy of life and success?

Yes   don't know/not sure   No

Everyone needs a set of principles to live by. Too many people, however, accept the values of others and never develop their own. They do not reflect enough upon their lives; instead, they worry about getting approval from others.

7. Are you taking the necessary risks to live your philosophy?

Yes   don't know/not sure   No

No one is ever completely sure of the path to follow, but those with the courage to believe in themselves and their ideas, with the potential of some loss involved, are the true individuals. You must take the risk – have the courage, to be true to yourself.

8. Do you feel a sense of meaning and purpose for your life?

Yes   don't know/not sure   No

Make a choice to focus your vigor on what gives you the deepest feeling. You can occupy your time and talents with people, commitments, ideas, and challenges that feel purposeful.

9. Do you have active goals this year relating to your purpose?

Yes   don't know/not sure   No

Purpose as a part of our lives serves as inspiration. But it is really our goals that motivate us on a day-to-day basis.

10. Are you living your life to the fullest now instead of hoping that things will work out someday?

Yes   don't know/not sure   No

Why let someone else decide your future? Use your potential now instead of taking it to the grave.

SCORE YOUR RESULTS AS FOLLOWS:

- For each yes answer give yourself a 0
- Not sure or don't know scores a 1
- Each no answer scores a 2

Now add up your score. As these questions are subjective, there are no right or wrong answers. However, use the scoring analysis as a general guideline. Here's how it works:

If you scored between 0-7, your life is pretty focused, you have a sense of direction, and you are intent on making a difference.

If you scored between 8-15, you have a sense of purpose, but you need to clarify your commitment. Are you really living your values and "walking the talk" every day?

If your score was between 16-20, you run the risk of not using your potential and just wasting your life. Please note: This high score may also mean that you are in the middle of a crisis or major transition.

ASSIGNMENT

1. Write a purpose statement related to your academic goals.

2. Write a purpose statement centered around your sports-performance goals.

To reinforce your purpose, embrace this statement everyday. Print it on a special card that you can keep close to you. Develop the habit of re-affirming your statement of purpose until it becomes totally ingrained in your consciousness. This is the catalyst that will change your behavior and allow you to actually enjoy living your life on purpose.

If you are not able to create a meaningful statement after doing this questionnaire, don't be too concerned. Often it takes several weeks to clarify this. What will help is to keep searching and thinking about what you are doing and why. The answers will eventually present themselves to you.

THE PURPOSE OF GOALS

Are you a conscious goal-setter? If you are, great. However, please read the information we are about to share. Chances are you'll benefit from the reinforcement, plus this expanded vision of setting goals may give you new insights.

If you don't consciously set goals, that is, you don't plan on paper or set targets for the weeks, months and years ahead, then pay very close attention to this information. It can dramatically improve your performance in the class room and in competition.

First, what is the definition of a goal? If you're not clear on this, you may get derailed before you start. We've heard lots of answers over the years. Here's one of the best:

A GOAL IS THE ONGOING PURSUIT OF A WORTHY OBJECTIVE UNTIL ACCOMPLISHED

Consider the individual words that make up this sentence. "Ongoing" means it's a process, because goals take time. "Pursuit" indicates a chase may be involved. There will likely be some obstacles and hurdles to overcome. "Worthy" shows that the chase will be worthwhile, that there's a big enough reward at the end to endure the tough times. "Until accomplished" suggests you'll do whatever it takes to get the job done. Not always easy, but essential if you want a life full of outstanding accomplishments.

Setting and achieving goals is one of the best ways to measure your life's progress and create unusual clarity. Consider the alternative – just drifting along aimlessly, hoping that one day good fortune will fall into your lap with little or no effort on your part. Wake up! You've got more chance of finding a grain of sugar on a sandy beach.

Choosing Goals Appropriate to You

How can we know what goals are appropriate for us? How can we be sure that the goals we choose suit our abilities, our interests, our overall purpose in life?

Goals are very personal. A realistic goal for one person is not necessarily a realistic for another. It may be entirely realistic for a budding young athlete to dream about becoming a gold medal sprinter in the Olympics. However, it is not realistic for a youngster who has lost both legs to set that goal.

Likewise, a goal which is appropriate for one point in our lives may not be at all realistic at another point. It may be fine for a sixteen-year-old to set a goal of becoming an astronaut but unrealistic for a fifty-five-year old.

SUCCESS IS THE PROGRESSIVE REALIZATION OF A WORTHY IDEAL

What goals are realistic for you now? What goals are reachable? Would the following high goals be appropriate, realistic, and reachable for you?

1. Winning the NCAA championship in tennis

2. Playing Division 1 college football

3. Signing a multi-million dollar sports contract during the next year

4. Scoring 2200 on the SAT

5. Becoming president of a Fortune 500 company

For most of you, these high goals are probably unrealistic. To some of you, one or more of them might qualify as appropriate. But what about these goals?

1. Scoring 200 points higher on the next SAT exam

2. Earning a 3.7 gpa or higher during the next semester

3. Starting your own company

4. Creating your own website

5. Sending your transcripts & highlights to 100 coaches and schools

A greater number of you probably felt that the second set of goals was more appropriate for you than the first.

FOUR QUESTIONS TO HELP YOU ACCURATELY CHOOSE GOALS

1. Is the proposed goal consistent with the way you see yourself?

2. Is the goal worthy of your very best efforts?

3. Is your goal consistent with your intuition and spirit?

4. Is your goal consistent with your values and purpose?

THE TOP-10 GOALS CHECKLIST

Here is a checklist to make sure you're using a successful framework to set goals. Pick out what seems to fit you best and use it.

1. Your most important goals must be yours.

This sounds obvious. However, a common mistake made by thousands of people across the country is to allow their main goals to be designed by someone else. This could be your coach, an instructor, your friends or family members.

2. Your goals must be meaningful.

When you prepare to write down your future goals, ask yourself, "What's really important to me? What's the purpose of doing this? What am I prepared to give up to make this happen?" This thinking process will increase your clarity.

3. Your goals must be specific and measurable.

Here's where most people lose it. It's one of the main reasons individuals never achieve what they're capable of. They never accurately define what they want. Vague generalizations and wishy-washy statements aren't good enough. Be more specific.

4. Your goals must be flexible.

Why is this important? There are a couple of reasons.

First, you don't want to design a system that is so rigid and cast in stone that you feel suffocated by it. Second, a flexible plan allows you the freedom to change course if a genuine opportunity comes along that is so good you'd be crazy not to pursue it.

5. Your goals must be challenging and exciting.

Many athletes seem to "plateau" once they reach high school, college, or the professional ranks. They lose the early excitement that was originally fueled by uncertainty and the risks involved to get to where they wanted to be.

6. Your goals must be in alignment with your values.

Synergy and flow are two words that describe any process moving effortlessly forward to completion. When your goals are in sync with your core values, the mechanism for this harmony is set in motion. What are your core values?

7. Your goals must be well balanced.

If you could start your academic and sports life over again, what would you do differently? When you're setting goals make sure to include areas that give you time to relax and enjoy the social aspects of life.

8. Your goals must be realistic

At first this sounds contradictory to the previous comments about thinking big. However, a measure of reality will ensure that you get better results. Where most people are unrealistic about their goals is in determining the amount of time it will take to achieve them.

9. Your goals must include contribution.

There's a well known proverb that says, "Whatever a man sows, that he will also reap." This is a fundamental truth.

10. Your goals need to be supported.

This last part of your goals checklist is controversial. There are three points of view. Some people advocate telling the whole world about what they are going to do. Here's the second option: Set your own goals, keep them to yourself and get on with the job. Third, and this may be the wisest strategy, selectively share your dreams with a few people you trust.

GO FOR THE GUSTO --- 50 GOALS

To get your juices flowing, make a list of 50 things you want to accomplish in the next 5 years. Have fun with this, and open your mind to all the possibilities. Create a child-like enthusiasm---do not place any restrictions on your thinking. Be specific and personalize your list by starting each sentence with "I am" or "I will." For example---"I will play college softball at Tennessee," or "I will receive a law degree from Yale University." To help you, here are a few important questions to help you focus:

- What do I want to do?
- What do I want to have?
- Where do I want to go?
- What contribution do I want to make?
- What do I want to become?
- What do I want to learn?
- Who do I want to spend my time with?
- What will I do to create optimal academic preparedness?
- What must I do to enhance my physical and psychological preparedness?

NOTES:

SPORTS MASTERY GOALS

KEYS TO MASTERY

1. Create a Picture Goals Book.

To improve your focus on the new academic and sports performance you want, create a picture book of your most important goals. This is an enjoyable process and the whole family can join in.

Buy a large photo album and start collecting pictures. For example, if your goal is to win the 100 meter state finals, cut out photos of your favorite sprinter crossing the finish line in first place. You can also find photos of him or her standing on the Olympic podium.

2. Use an Ideas Book.

This is simply a notebook where you jot down your day-to-day observations and insights. It is a powerful tool to expand your awareness. A brilliant idea without action is like playing baseball without a bat.

This is why an Ideas Book is so valuable. By recording your best thoughts in writing, you never need to rely on your memory. You can review your ideas anytime you want. Use your book for study group ideas, training ideas, class projects, college information, quotes you have read, or simple to-do lists.

Here's another valuable suggestion for your book. First thing in the morning, for ten minutes, record your feelings. Words to describe feelings include anxious, sad, happy, excited, bored, angry, enthusiastic, frustrated, energized.

3. Visualize, think, reflect and review.

Olympic athletes mentally run the event in their minds several times just before they perform. They totally focus on a positive result. Remember, if you copy the techniques of champions you too can become a champion. Use your positive imagination to create these winning pictures. The sharper these images are and the more intense you feel, the more likely you are to create the desired result. It's a powerful process. These techniques help to produce an unusual clarity, one that will give you a distinct edge in the classroom and in competition.

4. DEVELOP Mentors and Mastermind Groups.

Another wonderful way to insure major improvements in your productivity and vision is to enlist the aid of people who have vast experience in areas where you need the most help. When you surround yourself with a carefully chosen team of experts, your learning curve increases rapidly. Very few people do this consistently. Again, if you dare to be different you'll reap the rewards down the road. The alternative is to figure everything out yourself using trial and error. It's a slow way to move forward because you run into many roadblocks and distractions. On the other hand, cultivating advice and wisdom from specific mentors propels you to faster results.

A Mastermind Group consists of four to six people who meet regularly to share ideas and support each other. These are powerful alliances. They are designed to foster long-lasting relationships.

ACTION STEPS: YOUR PERSONAL MASTER PLAN

THE ACHIEVERS FOCUSING SYSTEM

Below is a complete review to help you implement your personal *"big picture"* Master Plan as well as your short-term action plan. To maximize your results, we strongly recommend that you schedule at least a half day to do this.

Top – 10 Goals Checklist

To maximize your results remember your goals must be:

1. Yours
2. Meaningful
3. Specific and measurable
4. Flexible
5. Challenging and exciting

6. In alignment with your core values
7. Well balanced
8. Contributing to society
9. Realistic
10. Supported

LIST YOUR CORE VALUES BELOW

e.g., Honesty, integrity, living a win-win philosophy, experience joy and happiness, learning from failure, accepting responsibility, being honest to thyself, learning from others, strong work-ethic,

forward thinking, accepts constructive criticism.

REVIEW

1. Your 50 Goals
2. Create a Picture Goals Book

3. Use an Ideas Book
4. Develop Mentors

MY PERSONAL MASTER PLAN

Sample sheet for 60-day goals. Create a similar worksheet for longer-term goals

SELECT YOUR TOP TWO ACADEMIC GOALS AND TOP TWO SPORTS-PERFORMANCE GOALS

FROM: _____ **TO:** _____

GOAL	SPECIFIC GOAL	REASON FOR ACCOMPLISHING	DATE ACCOMPLISHED
ACADEMIC	I will pass this term with a 3.8 gpa or higher.	To earn an academic scholarship for college	December 15, 2019
ACADEMIC	I will form a study group for Statistics and Calculus Class	To earn a bachelor of science degree in Exercise Science	November 9, 2019
SPORTS PERFORMANCE	Cut 40 yard dash time by 2/10 of second to 4.4	To start at varsity runningback	August 8, 2019
SPORTS PERFORMANCE	Complete Olympic Lifting Seminar	To familiarize myself with college strength training	August 2-3, 2019

THE ACHIEVERS FOCUSING SYSTEM

SELECT ONE GOAL IN EACH OF THE TWO AREAS. FOR CLARITY KEEP IT SIMPLE AND SPECIFIC.

THE SEVEN-DAY FOCUS: At the beginning of each week select the three most important things you want to accomplish. Choose activities that will move you toward the completion of your four major goals. Make contact with your mentor to review your progress.

FROM: _____ **TO:** _____ **MENTOR NAME:** _____ **PHONE #:** _____

WEEK	MENTOR CONTACTED	GOAL	SPECIFIC GOAL
1	YES NO	ACADEMIC	I will earn an A in my fall Calculus Class

1. Create study group for next weeks exam

2. Make flash cards for key terms & concepts

3. Meet with my instructor to discuss chapter 3 objectives

FROM: _____ **TO:** _____ **MENTOR NAME:** _____ **PHONE #:** _____

WEEK	MENTOR CONTACTED	GOAL	SPECIFIC GOAL
1	YES NO	ACADEMIC	I will score 200 points higher on my next SAT college exam in January.

1. Meet with SAT test prep Tutor

2. Study with group for 2 hours every Saturday until exam

3. Take a practice exam every Sunday until exam

FROM: _____ **TO:** _____ **MENTOR NAME:** _____ **PHONE #:** _____

WEEK	MENTOR CONTACTED	GOAL	SPECIFIC GOAL
1	YES NO	SPORTS-PERFORMANCE	Cut 40 yard dash time by 2/10 of a second to 4.4

1. Review starting block mechanics

2. Video 10 starts and analyse

3. Visualize starts for 5 minutes/daily

FROM: _____ **TO:** _____ **MENTOR NAME:** _____ **PHONE #:** _____

WEEK	MENTOR CONTACTED	GOAL	SPECIFIC GOAL
1	YES NO	SPORTS-PERFORMANCE	Complete Olympic Lifting seminar

1. Read & study the chapter on Clean and jerk

2. Watch and study 5 Youtube videos on the clean and jerk

3. Film and analyze my clean progressions

START 8 WEEK CYCLE

FROM: _____ **TO:** _____ **MENTOR NAME:** _____ **PHONE #:** _____

WEEK	MENTOR CONTACTED	GOAL	SPECIFIC GOAL
	YES NO		

1.

2.

3.

FROM: _____ **TO:** _____ **MENTOR NAME:** _____ **PHONE #:** _____

WEEK	MENTOR CONTACTED	GOAL	SPECIFIC GOAL
	YES NO		

1.

2.

3.

FROM: _____ **TO:** _____ **MENTOR NAME:** _____ **PHONE #:** _____

WEEK	MENTOR CONTACTED	GOAL	SPECIFIC GOAL
	YES NO		

1.

2.

3.

GOALS

FROM: _____ **TO:** _____ **MENTOR NAME:** _____ **PHONE #:** _____

WEEK	MENTOR CONTACTED	GOAL	SPECIFIC GOAL
	YES NO		

1.

2.

3.

FROM: _____ **TO:** _____ **MENTOR NAME:** _____ **PHONE #:** _____

WEEK	MENTOR CONTACTED	GOAL	SPECIFIC GOAL
	YES NO		

1.

2.

3.

FROM: _____ **TO:** _____ **MENTOR NAME:** _____ **PHONE #:** _____

WEEK	MENTOR CONTACTED	GOAL	SPECIFIC GOAL
	YES NO		

1.

2.

3.

FROM: _____ **TO:** _____ **MENTOR NAME:** _____ **PHONE #:** _____

WEEK	MENTOR CONTACTED	GOAL	SPECIFIC GOAL
	YES NO		

1.

2.

3.

FROM: _____ TO: _____ MENTOR NAME: _____ PHONE #: _____

WEEK	MENTOR CONTACTED	GOAL	SPECIFIC GOAL
	YES NO		

1.

2.

3.

FROM: _____ TO: _____ MENTOR NAME: _____ PHONE #: _____

WEEK	MENTOR CONTACTED	GOAL	SPECIFIC GOAL
	YES NO		

1.

2.

3.

FROM: _____ TO: _____ MENTOR NAME: _____ PHONE #: _____

WEEK	MENTOR CONTACTED	GOAL	SPECIFIC GOAL
	YES NO		

1.

2.

3.

FROM: _____ TO: _____ MENTOR NAME: _____ PHONE #: _____

WEEK	MENTOR CONTACTED	GOAL	SPECIFIC GOAL
	YES NO		

1.

2.

3.

FROM: _____ **TO:** _____ **MENTOR NAME:** _____ **PHONE #:** _____

WEEK	MENTOR CONTACTED	GOAL	SPECIFIC GOAL
	YES NO		

1.

2.

3.

FROM: _____ **TO:** _____ **MENTOR NAME:** _____ **PHONE #:** _____

WEEK	MENTOR CONTACTED	GOAL	SPECIFIC GOAL
	YES NO		

1.

2.

3.

FROM: _____ **TO:** _____ **MENTOR NAME:** _____ **PHONE #:** _____

WEEK	MENTOR CONTACTED	GOAL	SPECIFIC GOAL
	YES NO		

1.

2.

3.

FROM: _____ **TO:** _____ **MENTOR NAME:** _____ **PHONE #:** _____

WEEK	MENTOR CONTACTED	GOAL	SPECIFIC GOAL
	YES NO		

1.

2.

3.

FROM: _____ **TO:** _____ **MENTOR NAME:** _____ **PHONE #:** _____

WEEK	MENTOR CONTACTED	GOAL	SPECIFIC GOAL
	YES NO		

1.

2.

3.

FROM: _____ **TO:** _____ **MENTOR NAME:** _____ **PHONE #:** _____

WEEK	MENTOR CONTACTED	GOAL	SPECIFIC GOAL
	YES NO		

1.

2.

3.

FROM: _____ **TO:** _____ **MENTOR NAME:** _____ **PHONE #:** _____

WEEK	MENTOR CONTACTED	GOAL	SPECIFIC GOAL
	YES NO		

1.

2.

3.

FROM: _____ **TO:** _____ **MENTOR NAME:** _____ **PHONE #:** _____

WEEK	MENTOR CONTACTED	GOAL	SPECIFIC GOAL
	YES NO		

1.

2.

3.

SPORTS MASTERY

THE B-ALERT SYSTEM

Every well-built house started with a definite plan in the form of blueprints.

— Napoleon Hill

THE B-ALERT SYSTEM

The B-ALERT System creates optimal balance. It will help elevate your awareness and focus to a new level. This system can also be used as a tool to analyze daily behavior and motivation. We're going to analyze your daily behavior in detail, using the acronym B-ALERT. These six letters add up to a powerful formula that will help you create a well-balanced day. Repeat the process seven times and you'll have a well-balanced week. Persevere for just four weeks and you'll have a great month. Make it a habit every month, and before you know it you'll have a terrific year, with a lot more time off, and, a lot of academic and sports opportunities to go with it. As you go through each of the six steps, monitor your emotions. Be aware of any resistance you feel. Think about the reasons for this potential resistance. Letting go of any mental blocks will assist you tremendously in creating your new habit of optimal balance.

B IS FOR BLUEPRINT

This is how you prepare for the day. You do prepare, don't you? A blueprint is simply a map for the day. It helps you prioritize the important tasks on your agenda.

There are two options for preparing your blueprint for the day. Either do it the night before, or early in the morning before your day has started. You only need ten to fifteen minutes to do this.

Recent research indicates that if you create your blueprint the night before, rather than in the morning, your unconscious mind will actually work during the night figuring out how to fulfill your next day's plan, i.e., spell checking that essay, preparing the best science presentation, solving team conflicts, talking to recruiters and team tryouts, or solving any conflicts that need to be addressed.

So if you can, take time each evening to plan for the next day, and review your plan before bedtime. This review should focus on your most important activities, such as whom you will meet with and the purpose and objective of each appointment. Set specific time limits for your appointments. Also go over what projects must be worked on, and determine if you have reserved enough time to deal with them.

*It's important to have your own blueprint recording system. This could be a standard daily journal or time planner, or you may prefer an electronic organizer or software program to create your blueprint. Just choose a system that works well for you. For best results keep it simple. Customize it to suit your own style.

The one thing that separates winners from losers is, winners take action!

— Anthony Robbins

A IS FOR ACTION

When it comes to reviewing your results, the amount of action you put into your day will directly determine your score. Please notice, there is a major difference between being busy and taking specific, well-planned action. You can have a busy day with nothing to show for it. You didn't move closer to accomplishing your most important goals. The day just seemed to evaporate. Maybe you were dealing with little emergencies or you allowed yourself to be interrupted too many times. Do you see the big picture? It's better to invest your time in what you do best. Concentrate on the activities that produce the greatest results for you. Set limits on what you will and will not do.

All courses of action are risky, so prudence is not in avoiding danger (it's impossible), but calculating risk and acting decisively. Make mistakes of ambition and not mistakes of sloth. Develop the strength to do bold things, not the strength to suffer.

— Niccolo Machiavelli, The Prince

It isn't enough to think outside the box. Thinking is passive. Get used to acting outside the box.

—Timothy Ferris

L IS FOR LEARNING

Another feature of a well-balanced day is taking time to expand your knowledge. This doesn't require several hours of study. There are many ways to learn as the day unfolds. All that is required is that you be curious. Your level of curiosity about success in academics and sports-performance will go a long way towards helping you become successful. So let's look at some learning options. You can learn from books, audio recordings, videos and well selected media. Develop the habit of reading ten to fifteen minutes in the morning. It's a great way to start your day.

What should you read? Anything that is stimulating, challenging, or gives you the edge in the classroom or in competition. Biographies and autobiographies are particularly inspiring. Reading them will give you an extra boost of positive energy. *Whatever you do, avoid digesting any negative portions of newspapers. Loading up on wars, murders, riots, and disasters will only drain your energy before the day has begun--- not a good plan.

Also learn from yourself. You can gain a lot from your everyday experiences. How did you overcome your last challenge? Every time you take a risk or move out of your comfort zone, you have a great opportunity to learn more about yourself and your capacity.

Learn from others. You can learn a lot more by observing and studying other people. What do Rhodes Scholars do? What makes them successful? Why is your favorite star athlete successful? Why do some athletes continuously struggle throughout their careers? Using other people's experience as a yardstick for learning will help you tremendously. All you need to do is keep your ears and eyes open, and ask a few questions.

If you really want to rise to the top, invest one hour of your day to learn more about yourself and your competition. Developing this single habit can make you a world expert within five years. Remember, the use of knowledge is power. And powerful people attract great opportunities. This takes self-discipline, but won't the rewards be worth it?

E IS FOR EXERCISE

Exercise the body and the mind. Work on your squat mechanics. Brace the core, squeeze the glutes, screw your feet, and hinge the hips. Visualize the movement from start to finish.

Practice your wall march, fast-leg, and A-run drills. Focus on these cues: chin up, chest up, knee up, toe up, heel up. Remember…it's not what you do when the coach sees. What's more important, is what's done when the coach is not around.

Set a 30 day goal to train on your own two times weekly. Do whatever it takes to get through this critical time period. Keep these workouts limited to 1-2 movements or drills. Train no longer than twenty minutes. The key here is consistency and not being distracted. Have a no-exceptions policy, and give yourself a reward for not missing a single day. Learn how to train dynamically and consistently on your own. The point is, if you discover something that improves your performance, keep doing it. The rewards far outweigh the early discomfort. Stick with training on your own. The behavior of this habit will change your game.

R IS FOR RELAXING, REST, RECOVERY, REGENERATION

This is the time to recharge your batteries during the day. To avoid any potential rifts, schedule time for relaxing ten to fifteen minutes daily. The form of relaxing could be power naps, foam rolling for twenty minutes, stretching for 10 minutes, hydrotherapy, massage therapy, meditation, or taking a yoga class.

Looking at the bigger relaxation picture, how much time off do you take each week? And how many weeks per year do you schedule for fun? Let's define what time off is. If you plan to take one day off per week, make sure it's a full twenty-four hours. That means for a full twenty-four hours you do nothing related to studying, sports or training. The important thing is to develop the habit of creating real time for relaxing, rest, and regeneration. When you return from a week off, well-rested and refreshed, you will be more creative, stronger, better focused and more productive.

T IS FOR THINKING

This is a different kind of thinking. It's called reflective thinking. If you want to have unusual clarity about what is working and what is not working in your life, schedule time for reflective thinking. This is the final part of your B-ALERT system that will help you create an excellent balance every day. Here's how it works. At the end of your day, or just before you go to bed, take a few minutes to take a mental snapshot of the day. Regard each day as a mini-movie with you as the star. How did you do? Rerun the film and take another look. What did you do well? Are there any adjustments you could have made to create a better result? Focus daily on the progress you made. Be alert to any shortcomings, but don't beat yourself up. Learn from your mistakes. Be diligent. This only takes a few minutes each day, and it will make you stronger and wiser in the weeks and months ahead. You don't have to do everything in sequence. The flexibility allows you to be creative. Remember that creating a blueprint will save you time, because you have a clear picture of your priorities. By focusing on your most important activities during the day, you will be more productive and achieve greater results.

NOTES:

ACTION STEPS: THE B-ALERT CHECKPOINT SYSTEM

THE B-ALERT CHECKPOINT SYSTEM

This is a simple way to monitor your progress. It only takes a minute to check. At the end of each day ask yourself if you completed all six parts of the B-ALERT system. For example, if you had your blueprint organized, put a check mark through the letter B. If you spent the greater part of your day working on your most important activities, check the letter A. Repeat this for the remaining letters. Be honest with your evaluation. You will notice patterns developing each week that will highlight what you are doing right, and what needs to be corrected. Use a red pen to circle or line through the letters where your performance is lacking. For example, if you plan to work on your squat 10 minutes everyday, and you notice the letter E has five red circles drawn around it in the first week, you need to make some changes! As always, ease into this new habit. Don't be too hard on yourself at the start. The more practice, the better results you will have.

B-ALERT: A PROVEN SYSTEM FOR CREATING OPTIMUM BALANCE

BLUEPRINT

My strategic plan for the day. Priorities, appointments, projects. Review the night before or early morning.

EXERCISE

Work on those movements, drills, and skills that need more practice and development.

ACTION

Concentrate on the most important activities that will move you towards accomplishing your sixty-day goals.

RELAXATION

Eliminate daily stress. Nap, meditate, listen to music, foam roll, stretch, yoga, hydrotherapy, massage therapy, family time.

LEARNING

Expand your knowledge through reading, videos, mentors, courses.

THINK

Take time to reflect on the day. Review goals, visualize, develop new ideas, use a journal.

Track your progress every week. Set up your own simple recording chart, as in the example below. At the end of the day, take a moment to record your score. Circle any area that you miss.

MON	TUES	WED	THURS	FRI	SAT	SUN
B	B	B	B	B	B	B
A	A	A	A	A	A	A
L	L	L	L	L	L	L
E	E	E	E	E	E	E
R	R	R	R	R	R	R
T	T	T	T	T	T	T

MON	TUES	WED	THURS	FRI	SAT	SUN
B	B	B	B	B	B	B
A	A	A	A	A	A	A
L	L	L	L	L	L	L
E	E	E	E	E	E	E
R	R	R	R	R	R	R
T	T	T	T	T	T	T

MON	TUES	WED	THURS	FRI	SAT	SUN
B	B	B	B	B	B	B
A	A	A	A	A	A	A
L	L	L	L	L	L	L
E	E	E	E	E	E	E
R	R	R	R	R	R	R
T	T	T	T	T	T	T

MON	TUES	WED	THURS	FRI	SAT	SUN
B	B	B	B	B	B	B
A	A	A	A	A	A	A
L	L	L	L	L	L	L
E	E	E	E	E	E	E
R	R	R	R	R	R	R
T	T	T	T	T	T	T

MON	TUES	WED	THURS	FRI	SAT	SUN
B	B	B	B	B	B	B
A	A	A	A	A	A	A
L	L	L	L	L	L	L
E	E	E	E	E	E	E
R	R	R	R	R	R	R
T	T	T	T	T	T	T

MON	TUES	WED	THURS	FRI	SAT	SUN
B	B	B	B	B	B	B
A	A	A	A	A	A	A
L	L	L	L	L	L	L
E	E	E	E	E	E	E
R	R	R	R	R	R	R
T	T	T	T	T	T	T

MON	TUES	WED	THURS	FRI	SAT	SUN
B	B	B	B	B	B	B
A	A	A	A	A	A	A
L	L	L	L	L	L	L
E	E	E	E	E	E	E
R	R	R	R	R	R	R
T	T	T	T	T	T	T

MON	TUES	WED	THURS	FRI	SAT	SUN
B	B	B	B	B	B	B
A	A	A	A	A	A	A
L	L	L	L	L	L	L
E	E	E	E	E	E	E
R	R	R	R	R	R	R
T	T	T	T	T	T	T

MON	TUES	WED	THURS	FRI	SAT	SUN
B	B	B	B	B	B	B
A	A	A	A	A	A	A
L	L	L	L	L	L	L
E	E	E	E	E	E	E
R	R	R	R	R	R	R
T	T	T	T	T	T	T

NOTES:

SPORTS MASTERY
4 KEY AREAS OF ATHLETIC EXCELLENCE

FIVE KEY AREAS OF ATHLETIC EXCELLENCE:

If your performance slides into the dumpster, first explore the physical, technical, and tactical areas for solutions.

Physical

1. Body strength
2. Agility — your ability to change directions quickly and efficiently
3. Speed — how fast you can move from one point to another
4. Flexibility — your ability to stretch a distance or rapidly change muscle length without damaging your muscles
5. Endurance — the two energy systems in your body, anaerobic and aerobic

Technical

The technical arena of your sport refers to your mechanics and skill execution. It is, very simply, what you are able to do with your body — the form of your tennis stroke, the precision of of your glove work, the accuracy of your shooting, or your pitching mechanics, volleyball serve and ball handling. You develop good technique under the close supervision of a knowledgeable coach through countless hours of practice and repetition.

Tactical

The tactical part of your sport covers your knowledge of strategy and your ability to use this knowledge effectively by consistently making the right decisions under pressure. A volleyball player's ability to anticipate a developing play and move into position without the ball or a cornerback's skill of reading the opposing team's offense are good examples of tactical knowledge. Such knowledge is developed through good coaching, competitive experience, practice, studying film, and off-season training and conditioning.

Mental Toughness

The mental arena includes your abilities to concentrate, handle pressure, rebound from mistakes and setbacks, and avoid dejection and intimidation, as well as your confidence level, motivation, and preparation for competition. The volleyball player who comes up with a huge dig when her team has its back against the wall or the softball pitcher who strikes out three consecutive batters with the bases loaded, or the runningback with the winning touchdown after two previous fumbles are examples of athletes with strengths in this mental dimension. As with tactical acuity, mental toughness is developed through competitive experience, coaching, modeling of successful athletes, practice, visualization, setting goals, and reading.

These areas differ in importance, depending on the sport you play and your event or position within it. For example, in golf, the technical and tactical areas are absolutely critical, whereas agility, speed, and endurance play a much lesser role. If you're a sprinter in swimming or track, what's important is to go as fast as possible. Therefore, tactics aren't nearly as important as your technique, strength, power, speed, and endurance. If you play striker for your soccer team, your strength, agility, speed, flexibility, and endurance are as important as your technical expertise and tactical knowledge of the game.

While there is a constant interplay among these training dimensions, the mental arena provides the glue that holds the other three areas together. Regardless of the sport, what goes on in your head dramatically affects the physical, technical, and tactical performance by either enhancing or diminishing their effectiveness.

TESTING YOUR PERFORMANCE AWARENESS

So how do you determine the real culprit in your poor performance? Is it a physical, technical, or tactical factor? Or is it really your head that's wreaking all this havoc? Use the following questionnaire to help you answer this important question. Its purpose is to raise your awareness about your performance so that you can then make the needed changes to bust through poor performances. Keep in mind that awareness is the first step in change. Before you can fix any problem, you must become familiar with it.

For best results, first answer the questions by yourself. Next, ask a coach, parent, or someone else who knows your strengths and weaknesses to answer the questions. It is absolutely critical that you get input from someone besides yourself. Your own awareness is always limited.

To help you further determine whether your poor performance is being fed by some non-mental factor, get a coach or teammate to watch video of your performances. Watching yourself on video will help you see things that you might ordinarily miss. Comparing past and present performances can also help you identify what might be fueling the slump.

PHYSICAL, TECHNICAL, AND TACTICAL QUESTIONNAIRE

PHYSICAL

Is your poor performance caused by any of the following?

	WHAT YOU WOULD SAY	WHAT YOUR COACH WOULD SAY
Lack of sleep		
Lack of upper-body strength		
Lack of lower-body strength		
Limited agility		
Limited flexibility		
Poor endurance		
Slow foot speed		
Injury		
Sickness		
Inadequate diet		

TECHNICAL

1. Do you remember changing any aspect of your technique (for example: stance, technique, swing, stroke, stride, strike, follow-through, shot etc) before the poor performance started?

2. Have you deliberately changed any aspect of your technique since poor performance began?

3. Do you lack any specific skills that may be directly contributing to your performance difficulties?

4. Have you moved up into a higher competitive level recently?

5. What would your coach say about your technique and mechanics?

TACTICAL

1. Did you change any of your tactics before poor performance started? For example, a tennis player may decide to play more aggressively and attack the net instead of staying in the backcourt; a batter may decide to start pulling the ball more or go after the big hit every time up.) A cornerback may decide to play more aggressively by playing bump & run on every play.

2. Have you changed your tactics since poor performance began?

3. Have your tactics remained solid despite your bad play?

4. What would your coach say about your tactical grasp of the sport?

ARE YOU BURNED OUT?

In ruling out physical causes of performance problems, you need to consider one additional area. Poor performance can be a direct result of overtraining and burnout. If an athlete has been working too hard for too long without adequate rest, then performance will suffer. Chronic fatigue may set in, overuse injuries begin to surface, and performance gets stale. The athlete goes to practice or competitions hoping to just get through and counting the hours and minutes until it's over.

Poor performance can be a direct result of overtraining and burnout.

Rest is an important yet frequently overlooked part of training in every sport. *Athletes, distracted by a "more is better" philosophy of training, fail to adequately listen to their bodies. As a result they overtrain and allow their bodies too little recovery time. This flawed training regime results in diminishing returns — the more you put in, the less you get out. If your training or competition schedule does not allow enough time for you to recover, then the results often will be burn out and subpar performances.

BURNOUT QUESTIONNAIRE

Answer True or False to the following questions:

TRUE	FALSE	STATEMENT
		I am tired all the time.
		I don't enjoy practice the way I used to.
		When I practice, I frequently wish I were somewhere else.
		I dread competing.
		It has been a long time since I really had fun playing.
		I continually question why I remain in the sport.
		I find it hard to keep focused on my goals.
		I seem to get injured more than ever before.
		My injuries never seem to heal.
		My attitude seems to have become worse over the last several months.
		I resent having to sacrifice so much of my time for the sport.
		I don't handle the discomfort from hard training as well as I did last year.
		Sometimes I don't even care that I don't care.
		I'm more negative than usual about myself and my training.
		I have trouble concentrating in practice.
		I put myself down a lot lately.
		I really resent my coach.
		I have more trouble getting along with teammates than ever before.
		I feel pressured by others to remain in the sport.
		I don't seem to bounce back from setbacks and losses like I used to.
		TOTAL:

SCORING THE QUESTIONNAIRE

Each True = 1 point; each False = 0 points. Add up the total number of points. If you scored between 1 and 3 out of a possible 20 points, then you probably don't need to be concerned about burnout. Scores between 4 and 7 indicate that you're starting to "cook" and could use some time off. Scores between 8 and 14 indicate that you are in desperate need of a vacation from training and competition. If you scored 15 or higher, then you are seriously burned out and need to sit down with your coach and have a heart-to-heart discussion about your continued involvement in the sport.

STEP 2: ESTABLISHING SELF-CONTROL

To understand your poor performances and your role in it, identify what you are doing in your mind just before and during the performance — what you are thinking, focusing on, "seeing," and saying to yourself. Poor mechanics or tactics would quickly send your performance down the tubes; so too would poor mental mechanics or strategies. To break the cycle of poor performance, you must first recognize your counterproductive mental strategies and replace them with performance enhancing ones.

WHAT MENTAL STRATEGIES ARE YOU USING?

Part 1

Pick two or three examples of past competitions in which you clearly displayed poor performances. For example: In your last dual meet, you once again choked in the final 25 meters of the race. You struck out in the last inning with the bases loaded. You threw an interception when the game was on the line. You dropped a pass when the game was on the line. You lost again to the same opponent. You let a weaker player continually beat you to the ball.

Taking each performance separately, answer the following questions in as much detail as possible and record your responses: (answer these questions on a separate sheet of paper) Answer Questions 1 through 7 for each specific example of your poor performances. Compare your answers for each experience. Do you notice a common theme in your responses? Was your self-talk similar before each performance? Was your concentration focused on negative outcomes in each performance? Your thoughts, self-talk, focus, imagery, and expectations are your mental strategies for each performance. If your mental strategies are negative and self-defeating, they will keep you stuck with poor performance levels.

1. What were your thoughts and self-talk in the days leading up to and the day of the performance?

2. What imagery was in your mind before the performance?

3. What was the nature of your self-talk and thoughts right before the performance?

4. Did you have any pre-performance expectations? If so, what were they?

5. What thoughts and self-talk did you have during the performance?

6. When you made mistakes, what did you think and say to yourself?

7. What were your thoughts and self-talk after the performance?

Part 2

Pick two or three examples from peak performances when you were not struggling. You can include examples from parts of your game that are presently unaffected (for example, you're hitting in a hitting slump but your fielding is fine), you're running the ball well but at defensive back you're giving up touchdowns. Answer questions 1 through 7 for each of these positive experiences. Look for a common mental theme in these responses. What was your self-talk before and during these performances? Did you notice a consistent focus? How did you deal with miscues during these performances? Your thoughts, self-talk, focus, imagery, and expectations during peak performances are positive mental strategies that enhance performance.

Part 3

Compare the mental strategies you identified in Parts 1 and 2. What specific differences do you see in pre-performance self-talk and focus of concentration? Do you think and talk to yourself more when you are slumping? When the going gets rough during both good and bad performances, how do you handle the setbacks in each case? What do you concentrate on during a slumping performance as compared with a great one?

THE MENTAL STRATEGIES OF PEAK AND POOR PERFORMANCE

MENTAL STRATEGIES	POOR PERFORMANCE	PEAK PERFORMANCE
Thoughts	Negative, self-deprecating	Positive, supportive
Self-talk	Confidence-eroding	Confidence-enhancing
Focus	On uncontrollables	On controllables
Imagery	"See" what you're afraid of	"See" what you want

GETTING BACK IN CONTROL

Starting right now you can begin to take back control. You can learn to change those counterproductive mental strategies. Many of the thoughts that bounce around inside your skull give power and control to people and circumstances outside you. Getting back in control depends on your awareness of these thoughts and how much power you are unknowingly giving away. An important question to ask yourself here is, "How much am I participating in keeping myself stuck?" To find the answer, take the following short test.

Who's in Control?

Answer T if the statement is generally true for you or F if the statement is generally false.

1. I worry about my opponent's size, strength, or speed before I compete.

2. The temperature during the competition can negatively affect me.

3. When the conditions of the competition site are terrible, I tend to lose my confidence.

4. Faulty equipment or apparatus distracts me and hinders my performance.

5. Opponents who cheat have virtually no impact on me.

6. I perform better when people watch.

7. I tend to dwell on mistakes by the officials.

8. Overly aggressive opponents often take me out of my game.

9. A screaming, heckling crowd amuses me and I can easily forget about them.

10. I spend too much time wondering what the coaches think of me.

11. My coaches just seem to add to my performance troubles.

SPORTS MASTERY
QUESTIONS AND KEYS

TEN QUESTIONS THAT CAN CHANGE YOUR LIFE

The following questions can help you decide if you have what it takes to become a high achiever. They are designed to be seriously considered and answered from the deepest regions of your heart.

1. Do you really want to become a high achiever?

The key to all self discipline is desire. High achievers usually spend a great deal of time alone. Some people cannot tolerate solitude. A good index of your tolerance for being alone is the degree to which acceptance by your peers is important to you. High achievers are constantly finding themselves in new situations. High achievers must risk rejection by their peers.

2. Do you have a strong inner urge to reach out?

The urge to create, to achieve, to reach for new experiences is like a compressed spring inside the high achiever.

3. What matters most to you?
The key question for the high achiever is never What have you done? but What have you become? The real measure of the athlete is what the athlete values. What do you value most? Is it to start? Scholarship? Championship? Fame? Stats? Money? How much do you place upon the intangible qualities of life that are essential to becoming a high achiever? Some of these qualities are self-respect, pride of accomplishment, the capacity for teamwork, and a positive outlook. The path is often rough for the high achiever, and during those tough times you need more than material motivations to keep you moving.

4. What are you willing to invest? High
achievement requires an enormous amount of energy, time, effort, and commitment. One of the most self-defeating questions you can ever ask yourself is, How long will it take? The answer to that question is a little like the one given by the financier who was asked by a young executive who had seen the business tycoon's huge yacht, "How much does it

cost to buy a yacht like that?" "Young man," replied the financier, "if you have to ask, you can't afford it!"

5. How much are you willing to endure? "Life does not ask simply how much can you take? It asks, also, how much can you endure, and still be unspoiled?" wrote Harry Emerson Fosdick in the Manhood of the Master. In the same work he exclaimed, "What a testing of character adversity is!" Those who have what it takes to become high achievers learn to endure whatever difficulties they encounter, and they transform difficulties into opportunities. There is no room in the life of the high achiever for pettiness. It is destructive to complain about how you have been treated or what obstacles you have encountered.

6. What are you willing to give up? Everything around us is geared for comfortable living than high achievement. Once you decide to become a high achiever, you discover very quickly that you must constantly be willing to give up momentary pleasures and reach for long-term goals. Remember this: Whatever you give yourself to, it always becomes your master.

7. How much responsibility are you willing to assume? You won't find high achievers complaining about demanding practice schedules, year-round strength training, or practicing proper nutrition. You'll find them focusing their attention on how they can get better, or attaining a new goal. *High

achievement and responsibility go hand in hand. You cannot have one without the other.

8. Are you willing to start where you are? "A journey of a thousand miles begins with a single step," says a wise old Oriental proverb. How many hours each week are you spending developing your personal and athletic potential? Our dreams for high achievement can only become reality when we are willing to take the first small step toward fulfilling them. Remember this: You can always get to where you want to go, providing you are willing to start from where you are. Start doing what you can do, and then reach out for those things you cannot do now.

9. Are you willing to think for yourself? Someone once asked Joseph D. Kennedy, father of President John F. Kennedy, when it was that he started to make large amounts of money. He replied, "When I stopped pushing for it and went up and sat on the Cape and gave myself time to think." One of the great myths that keep people from becoming high achievers is the idea that the harder you work, the more you will accomplish. It is true that there is no substitute for honest, hard work. However, it is equally important to achieve a balance between thought and action. If you are willing to think for yourself rather than have someone else always do your thinking for you, you have what it takes to become a high achiever.

10. Are you willing to settle for nothing less than your full potential? Many people who have been high achievers are now failures because they refused to keep reaching out to become more than they were. "Success has ruined many a man," wrote Benjamin Franklin in Poor Richard. The person who reaches a modicum of success at an early age and spends the remainder of his or her life defending what has been gained must be considered a failure. High achievers continue to set very high goals for themselves — goals that are so high they can only be reached with the help of others. *If you are to become a high achiever, you must be willing to settle for nothing less than reaching your full potential.

MENTAL REHEARSAL

1 MUSCLE MEMORY

When visualizing, your brain sends signals to your muscles similar to the way it does during the actual sport performance itself - it helps your muscles "remember" how to move correctly.

2 AUTOMATIC RESPONSE

Practicing mental rehearsal can help you develp an automatic response to situations that may arise in your sport -- it helps you to simply react during competition, rather than overthink the situation.

3 ENERGY ZONE

Practicing mental rehearsal before practice and competitions can help you get in the right frame of mind - it helps you get into the right arousal state or "energy zone" by either relaxing your overanxious body and racing mind or energizing your fatigued body and lackadaisical mindset.

Please describe how incorporating mental rehearsal into your game plan will help you:

VISUALIZATION: 5 SENSES

99% of Olympic athletes use mental rehearsal techniques.

Please list a few examples of each sensory category (EX: I can hear the crowd)

HEARING:

SMELLING:

TASTING:

FEELING:

SEEING:

IMAGINATION — THE FIRST KEY

PRACTICE EXERCISE:

Picture yourself vividly as winning and that alone will contribute immeasurable to success. Great performers start with a picture, held in their imagination, of what they would like to do or be.

1. Set aside a period of 5-15 minutes each day where you can be alone and undisturbed. Relax and make yourself as comfortable as possible. Now close your eyes and exercise your imagination.

2. Imagine sitting before a large 80 inch screen and seeing yourself performing; be as vivid and detailed as possible.

3. To do this, pay close attention to small details, sights, sounds, objects, in your imagined environment. Details of the imagined environment are all important in this exercise, because for practical purposes, you are creating a practice experience.

4. During this 5-15 minutes see yourself acting, reacting appropriately, successfully, ideally. If you have been fearful and anxious in certain situations see yourself acting calmly and deliberately, acting with confidence and courage. This exercise builds new "memories" or stored data into your mid-brain and central nervous system. It builds a new image of self.

5. Do this everyday for 21 days.

KEY POINTS TO REMEMBER *(ADD THOUGHTS, FEELINGS, INSIGHTS, ECT. BELOW) LIST UP TO 21 BLANK LINES FOR CORRESPONDING DAYS*

1.

2.

3.

4.

5.

6.

7.

8.

9.

10.

11.

12.

13.

14.

15.

16.

17.

18.

19.

20.

21.

*Within you, whoever you may be, regardless of how big a failure you may think yourself to be, is the ability and the power to do whatever you need to do to be happy and successful. Within you right now is the power to do things you never dreamed possible. This power becomes available to you just as soon as you can change your beliefs.

SPORTS MASTERY

MASTERING THE UNCONTROLLABLES

MASTERING THE UNCONTROLLABLES

The uncontrollables are those things that you have no direct control over when you perform, but that most athletes invariably complain about: the officiating; the field and playing conditions; the weather; the time of day that you have to compete; the skill level, size, strength, and style of play of your opponents; your teammates; your coaches; the fans; parents' or others people's expectations; anything negative in the past, like a mistake, a previous failure, or an injury; and anything negative that might happen in the future, like losing or messing up. *As a general rule, a focus on uncontrollables will almost always set an athlete or team up for repeated failure. Such focus seriously erodes your feelings of personal power and causes choking and intimidation. Poor performance and uncontrollables go hand-in-hand.

Every time you're confronted by an uncontrollable, recognize it and quickly bring your focus of concentration back to what you can control.

While so many things are uncontrollable, the one thing that you can learn to control is your reaction. If you're presently struggling with poor performance, controlling your reaction may seem virtually impossible to you. But keep in mind that you maybe feeling so out of control mainly because of your mental strategy of zooming in on the un-controllables before and during performance. Un-controllables will continue to be part of the scenery of competitive sports. Re-establishing your control is about spotting un-controllables right away then deliberately steering clear of them by refocusing your attention on the things you can control.

Take a moment right now to think about your poor performances. Are you inadvertently feeding it by focusing on uncontrollables? If so, what specific uncontrollables haunt you? Write these down. Get to know them. Do you conjure up past failures before you perform? Do visions of possible mistakes dance in your head? Are you overly concerned about your opponents build and game stats? Do mistakes or bad breaks stick to you like glue? You will begin to regain your power and self-confidence as an athlete when you take control of the concentration piece of your mental strategies.

CULTIVATE SELF-CONTROL AS A WAY OF LIFE

Sometimes, as you set out to prepare yourself for high achievement, it seems as if everything around you is conspiring to keep you from reaching your high goal. But years of preparation, struggle, and exercise of self-control has taught us that there is a certain rhythm and harmony to life. The secret is to pick up on that rhythm and harmony and take advantage of the momentum it gives you, rather than fight against the elements you feel are seeking to control your life. Remember what St. Francis of Assisi said: "God grant me the serenity to accept the things I cannot change, the courage to change the things I can, and the wisdom to know the difference."

Cultivating self-control also means that you refuse to allow the opinions of others to direct you. Their opinions can affect you in two ways: (1) the flattery of people can make you lazy and self-satisfied, and (2) the disparaging remarks of others can discourage you and destroy your confidence. High achievers have learned to exercise self-control by ignoring flattery and weighing, not counting, their critics.

The masters of every art, sport, or skill make their feats look easy. Through long and arduous preparation, they have developed their technical skills and mental conditioning to the point that their actions have become natural responses. Not everyone can climb fast, but anyone can climb high. The high achiever learns to enjoy the climb because he or she knows that preparation is the path to great accomplishment.

WHICH SHOULD YOU FOCUS ON?

During the course of competition, many factors can affect your performance. some of these are:

IN YOUR CONTROL	OUT OF YOUR CONTROL
EX: energy level	EX: officiating
1.	1.
2.	2.
3.	3.
4.	4.

Here are some amazing and paradoxical secrets every high achiever must know:

1. It takes less energy to keep on climbing than to stop and hang on the ledge.

2. It takes less energy to go for the top than to wallow in the valley of frustration and anguish.

3. It's easier to contribute to life than to lie around.

4. It's easier to grow than to decay.

5. It's easier to prepare than to procrastinate.

Peak performance is exhilarating and exciting! The moment you begin your preparation, you will experience tremendous energy, and each step will take you nearer to the ultimate accomplishment of your high goal.

HIGH ACHIEVERS ARE WILLING TO RISK FAILURE

Failure can either be a weight, or it can give you wings. Thomas J. Watson, former president of IBM, has a simple formula for achieving success: Double your failure rate. The idea of succeeding by doubling your failure rate might sound strange to you. However, if you are going to be a high achiever, you must learn how to "fail" your way to achievement. Failing successfully is the only way to the top. Failure is not the enemy of success. It is a teacher – a harsh teacher, but the best!

Failure is a great character builder. It can give you strength to run and stamina to climb. I don't know of any high achiever who has not gone through the depths of failure. The secret is to learn from your failures. Every athlete has their share of problems and frustrations. High achievers recognize this as fact of life and don't let disappointments stop them in their efforts.

Here is a phrase you may have heard before: Anything worth doing, is worth doing well. But the high achiever says: Anything worth doing, is worth doing badly – at least at first. The first step upward toward your high achievement is the most difficult. It is the step most people will never take because they might not do it well the first time or even the second. To become a high achiever you must be willing to do it badly at first, and trust that improvements will follow.

WHEN A FAILURE IS NOT A FAILURE

You have only failed when you have failed to try. If you learn something valuable from your failure – if you develop strength of character – you can use it as a stepping stone along the road to high achievement.

Failures and disappointments put us under a great deal of pressure, but they also bring out strength, character, and endurance vital to high achievement. As an old proverb says: "A diamond is a chunk of coal that made good under pressure."

HOW TO HANDLE COACHES, PARENTS, THE MEDIA, AND FANS

- Don't waste your time and energy blaming others, even if you're right.
- Focus on what you can control, not what you can't.
- Ask coaches what you can do to turn things around.
- If your coaches are saying or doing something unhelpful, give them clear, respectful feedback on the impact of their behavior.
- If a coach is negative and unresponsive, find another coach who listens and can help you keep your perspective in dealing with the first coach.
- If your parents are saying upsetting things, be direct in telling them that their comments are not helpful. Then tell them exactly what you need them to say or do to be supportive.

- If your parents cannot be constructive, ask your coach for help.
- Remember to keep your goals in mind, not anyone else's.
- Don't allow yourself to get carried away with either positive or negative attention from the fans or media.

To get back in control, you need to keep focused on yourself and no one else.

SPORTS MASTERY
DEVELOPING
A CHAMPIONSHIP FOCUS

DEVELOPING A CHAMPIONSHIP FOCUS

In athletic performance, concentration is an important key to excellence. When you're ready physically and have the necessary experience in the sport, the outcome of your training rests almost completely on how and where you concentrate. Your concentration synthesizes all your training efforts into a laser-like point of energy that burns through obstacles and distractions to accurately zero in on the challenge of the moment. However, when it's misdirected or diffused, your competitive focus can weaken you, undercutting and neutralizing even the best of training regimes.

By learning to consistently control what you concentrate on, you can restore confidence, and unlock your peak performance. An athlete's or team's focus of concentration is an essential element in peak and poor performance. Your focus both before and during performance determines how well you'll handle pressure and influences the consistency and quality of your performance. A misdirected focus underlies almost all poor performances.

THE HERE-AND-NOW RULE OF PEAK PERFORMANCE

If you're stuck in a slump of poor performances, then learning to consistently focus on the current action of the competition is the next important step toward unlocking your game. The best way to do this is by understanding and using the here-and-now for peak performance. Simply stated, this rule says that to get the most out of practice and perform to your potential when you compete, you must mentally stay in the here and now of these performances.

When you're "on" and "in the zone" in competition, you are automatically concentrating on the flow of action. However, when you're "off" and struggling, you're violating this mental rule. Your head is everywhere else except in the here and now.

TIME

Concentration has two dimensions: time and place. When you practice or compete, you can mentally be in one of three "time zones": the past, present, or future. If you're in the past, your mind is behind your body — your body is performing now, but your mind is dwelling on something that previously occurred. For example, while you perform, your focus could be on a recent mistake, bad call, or missed opportunity. If you're in the present your concentration and body are in sync. Your focus is locked on to what you are doing at the moment. You watch the play as it develops to instinctively determine your next move, see this ball coming at you, feel the looseness of the bat in your hands as the pitch is delivered; or run toward the high bar, concentrating on your approach and then, at the perfect moment, switching your focus to your takeoff. If you're in the future, your mind is ahead of your body as you perform. You're thinking that unless you sink both of these free throws, your team will lose.

To consistently reach peak performance and your potential as an athlete, you must learn to consistently stay in the now of your practices and performances. *Choking in sports is all about being in the wrong time zone. Successful coaches know this and understand the critical principle of peak performance involved here: focus on the process, not the outcome. Pay more attention to giving a full effort and executing to the best of your ability. Narrow your concentration to the process of the game.

The concept of being in the now as you perform is very basic and something that athletes and coaches frequently overlook because of its simplicity. It is absolutely critical that you learn to recognize what time zone you're mentally in before and during performances. This awareness will help you head off disaster. Knowing, for example, that you tend to dwell on your past mistakes will help you recognize this disruptive time-zone shift and return your concentration to the now of performance. *If you spend several practices working on increasing your awareness of time zones and quickly returning your focus to the proper time zone as needed, then you'll begin to notice yourself doing this automatically when it counts in competition. Keep in mind that the basis for developing peak performance concentration and mental toughness is the ability to quickly recognize mental time traveling and immediately bring yourself back to the now of the performance.

PLACE

The second dimension of concentration: place refers to where you are mentally as you perform. Not only must you be focused on the right time, but you must also be in the right place. As you step up to take that penalty kick, are you thinking about how good the opposing keeper is? Are you watching the fans waving bright red towels and holding up their "air ball" and "choke" signs as you step to the free throw line to shoot those clutch free throws? As you move down the field, do you wonder what the coach thinks of your play? Are you preoccupied with those recruiters in the stands? Are you worrying about what your girlfriend or boyfriend thinks of you after that mistake? If you answer yes to any of these questions, then you were in the wrong mental place as you competed. To play to your potential, you must learn to keep yourself in the right mental place, "here."

In the space provided, list personal examples of when you were not mentally present for particular practices or competitions. What were your mental distractions?

When you're not in the here of the performance, it's almost impossible to play to your potential. Furthermore, you are far more vulnerable to the opposition's intimidation. Whether your opponent is deliberately trying to get in your head or not, to get psyched out, you must leave the here and focus on them. By learning to stay in the right mental place, you can minimize the psychological impact that your opponent's size, strength, speed, record, reputation, or behavior has on you. As an athlete, you can neutralize the effects of opponent's mind games by focusing on the game plan, and your job.

CONTROLLING YOUR EYES AND EARS

Besides developing first an awareness of when you leave the here and now and then the ability to quickly bring yourself back, what do you actually do to stay in the right mental time and place? Controlling your eyes and ears before and during competition is the answer. Before and during a game, you should look and listen to only those things that keep you calm, confident, and ready to perform to your potential.

*Athletes who have difficulty controlling their eyes and ears before or during performance invariably run into repeated performance problems. The inability to control your focus is what causes most poor performances and keeps them running. By learning to control where you focus your eyes and ears before and during competition, you will be well on your way to peak performance.

PRE-PERFORMANCE

Wandering eyes mean a wandering mind and frequently a self-destructive focus. Controlling your eyes entails locking your visual focus of attention on specific, prearranged points before your performance. Where you focus your eyes is especially important when there is a natural stoppage in the flow of performance, such as a timeout, a break between halves, or time between races, events, or shots. It is during these non-playing times when you have plenty of time to think that you're most vulnerable to a performance-disrupting loss of focus. As in all sports, the more time you have to get into your head, the more creative ways you'll discover to set yourself up for failure. Controlling your eyes pre-performance means that in the, minutes, and seconds before competition starts, you look only at things that keep you calm, loose, and confident. "Pre-performance" also includes the times just before you go to the foul line, set up for the field goal, when you're in the batters box, at the starting line for the 100 meter sprint. In short, you learn to control what you look at any time there is a break in the action and the flow is about to restart.

If looking into the stands or at your opponents makes you uptight, don't do it. Instead, find somewhere else to deliberately focus your eyes. Reading a book before or between events, watching your legs as you stretch them, picking out one spot and staring at it, looking down at your shoes, and focusing on your glove are all examples of what you can do to control your eyes. By picking specific targets to look at ahead of time and regularly using them, you'll have a much easier time successfully staying calm and confident when it counts. These visual targets or focal points will distract you from the real distractions.

Using the same focal points repeatedly will contribute to your comfort and confidence, because anything familiar tends to neutralize anxiety. It's the unfamiliar that causes athletes to get too anxious to play to their potential.

LIST EXAMPLES OF FOCAL POINTS

Like controlling your eyes, controlling your ears entails listening to only those things that keep you calm, confident, and ready to perform your best. To control your ears, you must learn to monitor two sources of auditory input: sounds coming from outside yourself, for example, the crowd, a teammate, or a trash-talking opponent; and sounds coming from inside yourself, your self-talk. Spend as little time as possible listening to things that drain your confidence. Many athletes control their ears by listening to music before the performance. Others repeat specific affirmations to themselves before they perform. For example, a high school sprinter might repeat to himself " explosive, powerful, super-fast." Affirmations can help counteract a negative mind-set and remind you of the right focus while simultaneously neutralizing old self-doubts and negativity.

Learn to monitor both sounds coming from outside yourself and sounds coming from inside yourself. A good ritual keeps athletes centered and focused in the here and now of the performance just before it begins. It keeps their minds off all the potential distractions and stressors within the competitive environment. The ritual provides them with a systematic way to gradually narrow their focus, so that when the action begins, they have perfect on-point concentration. The narrowing process is accomplished through paying attention to the focal points within the ritual.

DESCRIBE YOUR PREPERFORMANCE RITUAL

What can you do to improve this ritual and make it more effective?

*A word of caution here. Keep your rituals short and simple. Be sure that they involve things that are easy for you to do and don't depend on outside elements that you might not be able to control. You can always control warming up in a certain way, repeating certain phrases to yourself, and checking your equipment in a particular way. You can't always control having other people say or do certain things for you, eating a special   pre-game meal, having exactly one hour to warm up, or having your favorite bat available. Remember the ritual's purpose — to help you stay calm and focused and in control, not make you feel out of control.

DURING PERFORMANCE

When you run into challenging parts of competition, you need to have something positive and constructive on which to focus your concentration.

Many athletes use auditory focal points, like a verbal reminder, during a performance to block out other distracting, performance-upsetting noises. A softball pitcher repeats to herself the phrase "loose arms, now target" several times before every pitch. Within this phrase are two important cues that guarantee a fast and accurate pitch: The feeling of looseness in her arms helps her throw fast, and narrowing her focus to the catcher's mitt, her primary target for each pitch. By repeating this phrase mantra-like to herself, she is able to drown out the crowd's razzing and remind herself where to lock her concentration.

If you're the kind of athlete who is easily distracted by noise (a trash talking opponent, rowdy crowd, or plane flying overhead, try developing other sounds (internal or external) that you can focus on to counteract the distractions. These can be certain words that you repeat to yourself, a tune you play in your head, or some specific sound that is always part of your performance; your breathing, the oar movement as you row, the ball bouncing, or your foot strike while running.

DEVELOPING FOCAL POINTS

How do you decide what focal points you should use before and during performance? First, think back to some of your better performances. Can you remember what specifically you focused on right before the

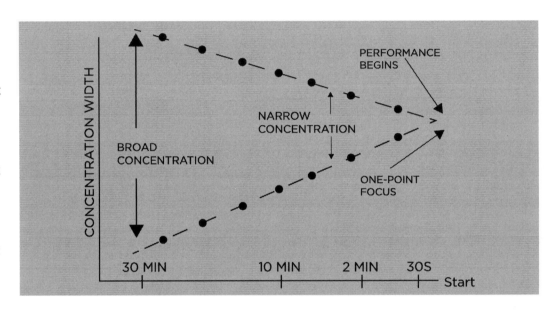

performance began (refer to the "What Mental Strategies Are You Using?" exercise discussed earlier)? Were you listening to music? Talking with friends? Mentally reviewing the upcoming performance? Stretching or warming up and focusing on how your body was feeling? Looking at something specific in the competitive arena? How about during the performance? What were you concentrating on? Was it a kinesthetic or body feeling (a feeling of the movement of your arms or legs as you executed)? Something that you visually locked your eyes on? A particular sound? Some combination of these?

By reviewing past peak performances in this way, you maybe able to discover some important clues as to what focal points best help you control your eyes and ears. To further help you do this, think back to some of your poorer performances and try to recall where your focus was for these before and during the action. Can you recall whether you were distracted by something visual ("I couldn't take my eyes off of how tall my opponents were")? Kinesthetic ("I felt so stiff and tight and I kept focusing on how bad I felt") Auditory ("This one guy kept razzing me every time I stepped up to the line, I couldn't get his voice out of my head")?

As you can see, focal points can be visual, kinesthetic, auditory, or some combination of the three. Based on your review of good and bad performances, can you determine which kind of focal point works best for you? If the size of the crowd or the appearance of your opponents during warm-ups tends to upset you, then develop visual focal points before the game to counteract those distractions. If negative self-talk, comments from the fans, or an opponent's verbal challenge bother you before the match, then develop auditory focal points. Similarly, if feelings of fatigue, stiffness, or low energy tend to fuel your pre game panic, refocus on different kinesthetic focal points (such as the feelings of stretching, warming up, or your breathing).

Developing performance focal points entails figuring out where your concentration needs to be to insure optimal execution. By examining your focus during past performances, you'll discover some of these focal points. Since peak performance is an unconscious process, you may not remember exactly what you were focusing on. Upon closer review, however, you should be able to identify specific visual, kinesthetic, and/or auditory cues that worked for you. For most athletes, focusing on a certain just-right feeling in their body as they perform (kinesthetic cue) leads to peak performance. The defensive back, sprinter, pitcher, volleyball player, and basketball player all intuitively zero in on a specific kinesthetic focal point when they are at their best. Similarly, many sports demand specific visual focal points (such as the ball, puck, or target) in the action for optimal performance.

*If you can teach yourself where to focus when under physical and competitive stress, and practice controlling your concentration in this way, you'll be far less vulnerable to mental breakdowns in the heat of competition.

NOTES:

SPORTS MASTERY
POSITIVE AFFIRMATIONS

DEVELOP POSITIVE AFFIRMATIONS

You don't believe in yourself. You feel that you don't belong on the team. You're not at all sure that you'll ever break out of your poor performances. Your negative self-talk brings you down and fuels your poor performances. One way to interpret this negativity and break down the walls of self-limiting beliefs is by using affirmations. An affirmation is a positive self-statement that you focus on and repeat to yourself many times a day. The power behind this technique is found in the adage, "You become what you think about most of the time." Few athletes can really believe an affirmation the first time they use it. With repeated practice, however, the positive self-statement starts to take hold.

In the space below, write the first thing that comes to mind in response to this question. The question is:

WHAT DO YOU WANT?

What thoughts occurred to you when you read the question? The question is easy to understand; it contains four simple words. Most people, as soon as they read the question, experience a flood of ideas, a rush of thoughts without order. In the confusion, they find it difficult to formulate a coherent answer. As a result, they give up and read on without answering.

This lack of clarity is precisely the problem. You do not know exactly what you want. You do not have a clear and specific image of your desires. This uncertainty is, by far, the number-one reason that most people are not happy or successful.

Suppose a man decides to take a plane trip for his vacation. He goes to the airport and the following conversation takes place between him and the ticket agent:

"Hello, I'd like to buy a ticket."

"Okay, fine. Where would you like to go?"

"Well, I'm not really sure."

"You want to buy a ticket, and you don't even know where to?"

"Yeah, I guess that's right."

"Well, I'm sorry, but I can't help you unless you know where you want to go."

"Oh, I don't really care, just someplace where I can be happy and have a good time."

"Sorry, sir. You need to know where you want to go. If you tell me that, I can get you there. Otherwise, I can't help you. I'd like to, but I can't."

This ridiculous conversation is the type of dialog most people have with their subconscious mind. Their mind would like to help them, but it can't. If they knew what they wanted, their subconscious mind could get it for them, but they haven't a clue about what they want. A philosopher once said that muddled thoughts mean a muddled life.

The first step toward getting what you want is knowing what you want.

*Realize that your subconscious mind does not respond to ambiguity. You must be specific. Get your pen or pencil ready. You will make two lists. The first list contains your most pressing performance problems. The second list deals with your ultimate performance solutions.

PERFORMANCE PROBLEMS	PERFORMANCE SOLUTIONS

Your first list is now complete. You have stated your immediate performance problems and compiled a list of acceptable performance solutions.

Now, you can have some fun. You can go wild on this next list. This time, list whatever comes to mind when you think of things/performances you want. This is not a list of what you need, but a list of what you desire. These can be performances you are nowhere near achieving at the present time. Look ahead and picture your game exactly as you wish it to be. Do not be timid. Do not limit yourself. Break records. Be phenomenal. If you can imagine it, list it.

WHAT DO YOU WANT

SELECTING THE WORDS...

An affirmation is a sentence that makes a specific statement about yourself as though the statement were already true. An affirmation is created for the purpose of implanting the expressed image into you subconscious mind. To be effective, an affirmation must be: (1) Specific (2) Positive

Both of these qualities are essential. First, an affirmation must be specific. The content of the affirmation must be expressed in sufficient detail for you to easily visualize it. When creating an affirmation, think of every possible aspect of the particular item. Include whatever details are significant to you and write them down.

Here is an example of an affirmation: "I, John, jump high." General "I, John, own a 36 inch vertical jump." Specific

To write a good affirmation, analyze and investigate. Decide on specifics. Do not write, "more play time." Be definite about your "play time."

Write, "I start at running back and defensive back."

In addition to being specific, an affirmation must be positive. Writing a positive affirmation is not as simple as it sounds or as obvious as you may think. Sometimes, an affirmation appears to be positive when it is not. For this reason proper wording is critical. An affirmation must be stated as though the fact were already accomplished. This requirement is vitally important. The wording may seem awkward to you at first, but you'll get the hang of it.

Let's say you want to run a faster 40 yard dash time. Your affirmation should read, "I Bryan, run a 4.38 forty yard dash.

Never write, "I John want to get faster." Your subconscious mind hears this statement and realizes that if you want it, you do not now have it. Thus, the image that gets implanted into your subconscious mind is: "I, John, am not fast." Notice that the result of this affirmation turns out to be negative. By the time the idea gets to your subconscious mind, it carries the exact opposite meaning from what you intended. Much of your thinking probably focuses on what you do not have. Your affirmations must not reinforce this thinking.

*The only form of affirmation that works is the form in which the item is described as though you already have it at this moment. Express your affirmation like this: "I, Morgan, throw 60 mph." Your subconscious mind hears this statement, and the image of 60 mph on the radar gun gets implanted. If you put your affirmations in this form, they will work.

*Do not use negative language in the wording of any affirmation. Avoid words such as "no," "not," "never" and so forth. An affirmation should describe something you want to attract, not something you want to avoid. Do not write, "I Leslie, do not have pain in my shoulder." Instead write, "I, Leslie, have cured the pain in my shoulder," or "I, Leslie, have a healthy shoulder that is free from pain." Always express your affirmations from a positive point of view.

In a sense, you are trying to "trick" your subconscious mind into believing that the thought expressed is true. That is easy to do if you word your affirmation properly. Your subconscious mind responds to clarity and assertiveness, not wishful thinking. That is why these two requirements — specific and positive are essential.

Create your own affirmations based on your unique desires. Let your individuality show when selecting the words. The safest policy is to use only affirmations that you invent. Those you create will work best for you. No generic affirmation, even a great meaningful one, can be as effective as one you devise yourself. Using affirmations you did not formulate does not engage your mind in the same way as using ones you did.

Your affirmations are unique. Your innermost thoughts and desires are a reflection of you, alone. You are not a generic person.

I run fast

I jump high

I am a great athlete

I am a fierce competitor

I can run like the wind

I am a winner

I have great stamina

I am dedicated to my training

I am motivated to practice

I am a skilled player

CREATING YOUR AFFIRMATIONS

You are now ready to create your affirmations. Write all affirmations in the following form:

I, (your name), (the affirmation).

1.

2.

3.

4.

5.

6.

7.

8.

9

10.

Now that you have your list of affirmations, here's how to get the images implanted into your subconscious mind. Do the following three things every day.

FIRST: Immediately upon awaking in the morning, read your affirmations out loud and visualize them. Take your page of affirmations and, starting at the top, read through the entire list. Read each affirmation clearly. Pronounce every word slowly and distinctly. Be audible and listen to your voice. Do this soon after waking, when your mind is still impressionable. A while after you wake up, your mind enters full waking consciousness and becomes less receptive.

SECOND: Once during the day, write one of your affirmations repeatedly. You can do this anytime — morning, afternoon or evening — whenever you have a pencil and paper and a few uninterrupted minutes. (Some people ask if they can write their affirmations during the same session when they do their reading. The answer is yes, provided the timing is convenient for them. Many people prefer doing it then.)

Pick one of your affirmations. You can choose one you particularly want to work on or one you haven't put much effort into lately. You can pick the same one several days in a row or a different one every time. Once you've made your selection, write the affirmation over and over. You should write

it a minimum of ten times. Twenty times is even better. The more times you write an affirmation, the more quickly you see results. Do not overdo it though. Never write to the point of experiencing writer's cramp.

THIRD: Read your affirmations out loud and briefly visualize each one. This should be the last thing you do before retiring at night. It is an exact repeat of the morning procedure.

Try to do this reading as close as possible to the time you fall asleep. The same considerations apply here as apply to your morning reading. If you sleep alone, you should have no problem reading your affirmations out loud in bed before you doze off. If you sleep with another person, you may prefer to read privately somewhere else in the house before climbing into bed. The details are up to you. This three-part procedure requires less than ten minutes per day.

Ralph Waldo Emerson said, "A man is what he thinks all day."

NOTES:

DAILY ACTIVITIES

MONTH:_____ **YEAR**_____

First: Morning Reading and Visualization, Second: Writing (one affirmation only), Third: Evening Reading and Visualization

AFFIRMATIONS PERFORMANCE CHART

DAY	FIRST	SECOND	THIRD	COMMENTS

DAY	FIRST	SECOND	THIRD	COMMENTS

WHAT YOU SHOULD NEVER FORGET ABOUT BELIEF

1. Imagination is more important than knowledge. If you can't visualize it happening, it will not happen. Anyone wanting to break records and push boundaries must build a clear picture in their mind of what they want to achieve.

2.Too much information and knowledge can limit potential, paralyze action and kill belief. A top performer must distinguish between what they really need to know and what is nice to know.

3. Belief is not about being right. It's about winning. What often separates the best from the rest is a capacity to believe things that are logically not true, but which are powerfully motivating.

4. Be realistic, but be unrealistic at the same time. Any organization wishing to deliver high performance must nurture its ability to think on an unrealistically large scale and stimulate its naivety about what's possible.

NOTES:

SELF-REPORT REVIEW

Upon completion of the workbook, please complete the self report review questions below by marking an X in the appropriate box.

USING TECHNIQUES OUTLINED IN:	YES, CONSISTENTLY!	SOMETIMES	NO, STILL A WORK IN PROGRESS
1= I can generate positive self-talk statements.			
2= I can create a personal goal.			
3= I can incorporate mental rehearsal techniques.			
4= I can improve my self-confidence.			
5= I can mantain a more mentally tough approach.			
6= I can increase my motivation.			
7= I can describe how life skills are learned through sports mastery.			

EPILOGUE

Everyone holds his fortune in his own hands, like a sculptor the raw material he will fashion into a figure. But it's the same with that type of artistic activity as with all others: We are merely born with the capability to do it. The skill to mold the material into what we want must be learned and attentively cultivated.

— **Johann Wolfgang von Goethe**

There exists a form of power and intelligence that represents the high point of human potential. It is the source of the greatest achievements and discoveries in history. It is an intelligence that is not taught in our schools nor analyzed by professors, but almost all of us, at some point, have had glimpses of it in our own experience. It often comes to us in a period of tension---facing a deadline, the urgent need to solve a problem, a crisis of sorts. Or it can come as the result of constant study and training. In any event, pressed by circumstances, we feel unusually energized and focused. Our minds become completely absorbed in the task before us. This intense concentration sparks all kinds of ideas---they come to us as we fall asleep, out of nowhere, as if springing from our unconscious. At these times, other people seem less resistant to our influence; perhaps we are more attentive to them, or we appear to have special power that inspires their respect. We might normally experience life in a passive mode, constantly reacting to this or that incident, but for these days or weeks we feel like we can determine events and make things happen.

We could express this power in the following way: Most of the time we live in an interior world of dreams, desires, and obsessive thoughts. But in this period of exceptional creativity, we are impelled by the need to get something done that has a practical effect. We force ourselves to step outside our inner chamber of habitual thoughts and connect to the world, to other people, to reality. Instead of flitting here and there in a state of perpetual distraction, our minds focus and penetrate to the core of something real. At these moments, it is as if our minds---turned outward—are now flooded with light from the world around us, and suddenly exposed to new details and ideas, we become more inspired and creative.

Once the deadline has passed or the crisis is over, this feeling of power and heightened creativity generally fades away. We return to our distracted state and the sense of control is gone. If only we could manufacture this feeling, or somehow keep it alive longer…but it seems so mysterious and elusive.

The problem we face is that this form of power and intelligence is either ignored as a subject of study or is surrounded by all kinds of myths and misconceptions, all of which add to the mystery. We imagine that creativity and brilliance just appear out of nowhere, the fruit of natural talent, or perhaps of a good mood, or an alignment of the stars. It would be an immense help to clear up the mystery—to name this feeling of power, to examine it's roots, to define the kind of intelligence that leads to it, and to understand how it can be manufactured and maintained.

Let us call this sensation mastery: the feeling that we have a greater command of reality, other people, and ourselves. Although it might be something we experience only for a short while, for others ---Masters of their field---it becomes their way of life, their way of seeing the world. (Such Masters include Leonardo da Vinci, Eric Thomas, Dan Gable, Robert Greene, Kobe Bryant, Less Brown, Aaron Draplin, Simon Sinek, Anderson Silva, Tony Robbins, Floyd Mayweather, Curtis Jackson, Richard Sherman, Usain Bolt, David McHenry, Kenny Austin, Leland Johnson, Bruce Lee, Leslie Poole, Mike Hubbell, Muhammad Ali, Mozart, MC Escher.

DESHAWN FONTLEROY

DeShawn Fontleroy, RBT, FMS is a USA Track and Field Coach, USAW Sports Performance Coach, and Founder of Proforce Athletics. He specializes in problems of training--including the role of speed-specific strength training, explosive power development, and sprint training in athlete's physical preparation. His programs are compounded and melded with sport-psychology and sociology of sport. DeShawn has facilitated lectures and seminars concerning the theory of sports training. He has also worked with professional football, hockey, and MMA athletes.

SUGGESTED READING AND ADDITIONAL RESOURCES FOR SUCCESS

1. The Art of Possibility, by Rosamund Stone Zander and Benjamin Zander, New York, Penguin, 2000

2. The DNA of Success, James A. Ray, La Jolla, Calif.: SunArk Press, 1999

3. The Success System That Never Fails, by W. Clement Stone, Englewood Cliffs, NJ: Prentice-Hall, 1977

4. Napoleon Hill's Keys To Success, edited by Matthew Sartell, New York: Plume, 1997

5. What Makes The Great Great, by Dennis P. Kimbrow, Ph.D New York: Doubleday, 1997

6. The Seven Habits of Highly Effective People, by Stephen R. Covey, New York: Fireside, 1989.

7. Play To Win, by Larry Wilson and Hersch Wilson, Austin, Tex: Bard Press, 1998

8. The Magic of Believing, by Claude M. Bristol, New York: Simon & Schuster, 1991.

9. The Power of Positive Habits, by Dan Robey, Miami: Abritt Publishing Group, 2003.

10. The Magic of Thinking Big, by David Schwartz, New York: Fireside, 1987

11. Success Through a Positive Mental Attitude, Napoleon Hill and W. Clement Stone, Englewood Cliffs, NJ: Prentice-Hall, 1997

12.. The Traits of Champions, by Andrew Wood and Brian Tracy, Provo, Utah: Executive Excellence Publishing, 2000